BUDGETING

A Practical Guide to Managing Your Money the Minimalist Way

(How to Take Control of Your Money, Reduce Debt and Start Living)

Samuel Barraza

Published By Jackson Denver

Samuel Barraza

All Rights Reserved

Budgeting: A Practical Guide to Managing Your Money the Minimalist Way (How to Take Control of Your Money, Reduce Debt and Start Living)

ISBN 978-1-77485-263-7

All rights reserved. No part of this guide may be reproduced in any form without permission in writing from the publisher except in the case of brief quotations embodied in critical articles or reviews.

Legal & Disclaimer

The information contained in this book is not designed to replace or take the place of any form of medicine or professional medical advice. The information in this book has been provided for educational and entertainment purposes only.

The information contained in this book has been compiled from sources deemed reliable, and it is accurate to the best of the Author's knowledge; however, the Author cannot guarantee its accuracy and validity and cannot be held liable for any errors or omissions. Changes are periodically made to this book. You must consult your doctor or get professional medical advice before using any of the suggested remedies, techniques, or information in this book.

Upon using the information contained in this book, you agree to hold harmless the Author from and against any damages, costs, and expenses, including any legal fees potentially resulting from the application of any of the information provided by this guide. This disclaimer applies to any damages or injury caused by the use and application, whether directly or indirectly, of any advice or information presented, whether for breach of contract, tort, negligence, personal injury, criminal intent, or under any other cause of action.

You agree to accept all risks of using the information presented inside this book. You need to consult a professional medical practitioner in order to ensure you are both able and healthy enough to participate in this program.

TABLE OF CONTENTS

Introduction

There is no need to convince you of the benefits of financial wellbeing. There are many of them, and some even seem to be awe-inspiring. People who are able to manage their money enjoy a happier life, and also live for longer. They enjoy better living conditions and have more success. The way you manage your money is more than the amount of money of your savings account or credit score. It's about the way you live your life.

A bad credit score and debt are all things which can be fixed. Fortunately, it's not too difficult. The cause of financial stress is usually due to bad habits that we were taught from the age of a child. But the good news is that we can re-learn these damaging ways of life and become independent. The constant worry about money isn't a good way to live your life. It's an obligation that takes the fun out of life and takes it out of your life. It must be ended not later and not later, but right today.

I will provide strategies and tips that can transform your financial situation. We will discover how to budget your money and change your spending habits to increase credit scores, and keep your financial independence. If you follow my advice you will see your life take on a new dimension you've never imagined. You'll radiate wealth as well as confidence and joy.

The tools that are in this book are those I've used myself and I am able to swear to the tools. I have employed these tools to ease financial burden, spend prudently and to save. People I have met expressed gratitude to my for teaching these easy techniques because they changed their lives. I was taught these strategies at an early age. I was fortunate enough to have a mom who was excellent in dealing with money. I was taught these techniques. The way I manage on my finances, saving and budgeting are the things she taught me.

Today, I own an account on a credit card and an rating of 700 on my credit report and I'm just in college!

These suggestions are universal. It doesn't matter how young or old you are. They were employed by my mother. They are now working for me and work for my friends as well as many others. They will also do their best to your benefit. You have earned financial freedom as well as all the advantages it can bring. It's about time to take it for granted.

Let's start that journey.

Chapter 1: Budgeting 101

"Don't reveal what you value. Instead, show me your budget and I'll tell me what you appreciate."

Joe Biden

Budgeting is one of the things that people are not taught how to perform. Reviewing expenses and income isn't fun, especially in the case of feeling guilty for spending more than you should.

Before we look back at the things that have been going on in the past, make a conscious effort to be compassionate to yourself. Let yourself be sorry for any mistakes you've made in the past . Then be proud of these courageous steps you're taking to provide you and your family financial security.

Are you prepared? Let's get started on with budgeting!

The first thing you should do is record everything you've spent the past month. It might not be simple but try your best. The goal is to have an understanding of how much money you are spending to allow you to make changes.

After you've jotted down the areas you used your money, you're planning to have a examination of the various areas you spend money on and decide what you could reduce and what you could eliminate. Here are some suggestions to help you create an achievable budget for yourself.

A cautionary note. When making your budget, be flexible! If you're too strict on your budget, you'll be sabotaging your efforts. It is important to have fun in life, so be sure there's a small amount to be set aside for fun and entertainment. This will make it easier to stay within your budget.

Take note of where you're spending your money, particularly on unnecessary things.

What are you able to cut out or substitute for a more cost-effective alternative? A lot of bars and restaurants are included in this category. If you invite your friends instead of dining out. You'll save many dollars. Instead of sending your kids out to the cinema or to the cinema, you can rent a film (or even better, purchase an item from your library) and cook pizza in your home.

A few guidelines on where you should spend your money include 50% of fixed expenses 20% on long-term financial goals, and 30% for flexible spending.

Fixed costs are those which don't change between months such as rent or mortgage payment, car loans and utility bills. Other items that fall under this category and could be cut off temporarily include memberships to gyms and online accounts such as Netflix or Gamefly and subscriptions to magazines. Make sure to reduce this category of budgeting down to less than 50%, and then put the money you can spare towards the repayment of debt.

The long-term financial goals include the savings and investments that can secure the financial security of your future. The three main pillars in this chapter are getting rid of the debt as well as saving for retirement and establishing the emergency funds. We'll go into more detail about the emergency fund later in the chapter. After you have gotten rid from debt, it is possible to are able to also add larger purchases, such as a downpayment on the house or an upgrade to your automobile. I strongly recommend making your savings automated so you never get the chance to spend your cash. There are programs to consider such as Digit or SmartyPig to find out which is the best for you.

Then, you can consider flexible spending as the daily costs that you'll be able to cut to a minimum. It includes eating out, purchasing new clothes or hobbies, grocery shopping and other forms of entertainment. While food items are necessary but there's plenty of freedom in what you buy. It is possible to spend a significant amount for meals that are already prepared or you can pay less by cooking from scratch. The lower your expenses here, the more quickly your debt will be paid off.

The aim of your budgeting stage is to reduce the most amount you can, but be honest about how much you'll have to pay. It's a delicate balance and can take a couple of months to master. As long as you begin by making every minimum payment and establishing an emergency fund, you'll get on the proper path. As each month passes you will be able to make more adjustments to your plan.

Chapter 2: Follow The Money

There's a saying: the failure to plan means planning to fail.If you aren't able to see the direction you're headed and how to get there, what are the best ways to reach your goal? The most powerful corporations around the globe have budgets and plans to manage their finances.As the truth is every business, big or small, that's committed to success has a budgeting procedure.

A lot of people are afraid about budgeting due to two primary reasons.First they feel it's a difficult process and secondly, they believe that it's a lengthy task that's not worthwhile doing.Some might have jobs in companies with entire departments that are tasked with preparing budgets. The prospects of doing it by themselves seem difficult.

Then you'll be able to master this skill within a matter of minutes, so put on your shoes.

Basic concepts and terminologies

Before we move on to the steps, remember you are creating a MAP which outlines your future plans by dividing them into dollars and cents.You will be witnessing your financial "life" unfold in front of you.Best is that you are in control of your financial situation, and not be influenced by the same forces that were previously able to control you.

Every budget is comprised of two parts which are money that you put into (or earn) (income) and the money that you pay out (expenses).

The objectives that the budgeting process is attempting to achieve are

(1) Be sure that at the at the end of every month, we have money left for savings.

(2) Controlling and monitoring your expenditure.

Costs are further broken down into variables or fixed expenses.The distinction is essential in planning the coming expenses.A fixed cost is a sum that you use every month, no regardless of what.It does not change regardless of the things you do.These are the expenses are beyond your control over at least not in the short-term, and they are required to be paid for regardless of what.

These are fixed costs you'll need to keep track of:

Rent

Mortgage payments

Car loan payments

Tuition/day care/babysitting

Student loan repayments

Other fixed loan repayments like installment charges on lines of credit or furniture and appliances

Tax installment payments

Credit card transactions (more on this in the future!)

Utility bills - Even though gas, electricity water, phone bills change each month, you know you'll have to pay them.These include charges for pest control and garden work are contracted out.

Premiums for insurance (health life, automobile insurance)

Taxes on property

Activities and lessons for children

It is important to note that some of these expenses, though fixed, are not always to be paid monthly.Many Tax bills can be paid out quarterly, semiannually as well as annually.Health health insurance costs are typically paid in a quarterly fashion most of the time.You must think about this as you move along.

Variable expenses are the amount of money you have the option of spending or select the amount you want you want to spend.This covers virtually all other expenses that you do not categorize as a fixed expenditure.

Variable costs typically comprise the following:

Groceries

Medicines, personal care items and other items

Fuel/Gasoline

Parking and tolls

Clothing

Work lunches, coffee, & snacks

Restaurants and eating out

Entertainment (movies, shows, spectator sports)

Tobacco / alcohol

Medical expenses out of pocket

Public transportation (bus, trains, etc.)

Lottery and gambling

Magazines / newspapers / books (regularly scheduledsubscriptions may be classified as fixed)

Haircuts/treatments at the beauty salon and other services

Contributions to religious or church organizations/tithes

In general If you aren't sure what to do with expenses, it's considered a variable expense.If you are able to count on tiny expenses for specific items like printer cartridges, as well as parking and tolls for instance, could be classified with the supplies as well as transportation or car expenses, for example.

Sort and organize your files

Then we can get to the exciting part.Actually creating your budget! The first thing you must do is gather all pay slips and other documentation to prove the amount of amount of income you received.This might include bank statements for the interest you earn from deposits and direct deposit of wages as well as commissions and bonuses.

The majority of the work during this process involves assembling statements from banks and credit card statements, receipts, bills, and each piece of paper or document that will prove the things you've paid for.You may also want to print any emails that are related to the financial transaction, like acknowledgment of a purchase to be made.

To be able to use our services for our purposes, you must have at least three months' worth of data.

With your credit card and statement from your bank (from you ATM credit cards),

PayPal statements or any other summary you receive that contain information about expenses, make sure you mark every item that reflects the cash flow outgoing for all types of expenses that you've made.

The reason to do this is because you want to establish a foundation to calculate your earnings and expenses.Laying out what you've performed in the previous years is crucial to plan your future.

Then, you must organize all the files into 3 groups or piles, if you prefer:

The income pile

A fixed cost pile

The variable cost pile.

If you're confident in your ability to have the details readily available, you are able to make use of the spreadsheet later in this chapter, to track the cost.

Chapter 3: Identifying Your Personal Motivational Sources

You have to be the one to find out the reasons that drive you to make a budget and reduce expenses. You should already have an incentive to purchase this book. It is time to awaken your motivation right now by answering the following question:

What are the reasons you'd like to budget your funds?

If none of that helps to narrow the issue, you can narrow the search by selecting one of these questions:

Who is the person who motivates you to save and budget?

What are you planning to buy if successful in saving money and budgeting?

When you reflect on these questions, you'll be able to identify your own personal motivation for budgeting. Write your motivation in the form of your dream statement. It is a phrase or paragraph that reminds you of the reason behind making a budget.

Many people plan to save money for a costly purchase. Some prefer spending big for experiences such as trips to places that are unique all over the world. For many, their main motivation lies close to their home. They wish to save enough money for their children a the best college education.

If you are writing your personal statement of your dreams it is important to personalize it with the right words. You must make use of specific phrases. Instead of using the phrase:

I'd like to save to fund my son's college tuition.

You could declare:

I am saving money for Michael's education at MIT. MIT.

This is a message sent from your young self towards your elder self. When you use the child's name it gets more personal each time you listen to it. We also altered the tense in the phrase. We removed the future tense and switched it to the present tense. This means that you are already performing the task. Budgeting begins the moment you set your goals and record it on paper. It is not a matter of stopping until you have reached your objectives.

Write your dream declaration on multiple pages. It is recommended to tape a statement to all of your credit cards. It is also advisable to keep an original copy of the statement inside your wallet. It should be easily accessible when you go to open your wallet. It is a way to remind yourself of the things you're saving each time you go to your wallet. Most likely you'll be able to be able to make better financial choices whenever you look at these reminders. This strategy will only work when you don't pay attention to your ideal statements once you have them. You must make it a habit to read your statement in front of you when you notice it.

Create a habit of self-talk

A majority of people buy items on impulse. They don't put in much thought into buying. If you are inclined to be the same way then you need to develop the habit of thinking and stopping prior to making purchases.

You don't have to create a complex argument for each purchase. All you need to do is consider this before you make a purchase:

Am I making a prudent choice?

It is best to answer this question by speaking to yourself loudly. We are more likely to make better decisions when we understand our own reasons for our choices. It's also less difficult to deceive yourself if we only use our brain to justify the purchase. We often feel embarrassed of our actions when we are told that.

Chapter 4: Tools for Budgeting

There are many budgeting tools in the market today. Being able to choose from a variety of options is wonderful, but they can be overwhelming, especially when you consider the fact that every budget will differ.

The program You Need a Budget is available on your computer's desktop, Android device, and iOS device. If you install it on every device it can be a very powerful tool you can utilize to keep your financial data on ready for when you require it. The mobile application allows you to sync your budget information (from your desktop) and input any every time you make a transaction check how much of your budget is at your disposal and let you look back at your transactions history and a categorical budget. The catch is that the mobile apps are free, but the desktop version is expensive. Of course, you'll require the desktop version to utilize the apps, so... But there's a free trial available on their website , so you can test whether it is the software will help you remain on your budget.

Home Budget with Synchronization is now available on each of the Android as well as iOS platforms at a cost of $5. It's a budgeting and expense management tool you can use to transfer financial data between various devices. You can make an account of your budget, track and categorize expenses, monitor your income and track the amount you spend. Through analyzing the data you will be able to learn more about the habits you make with your money. The app makes it simple by providing you with infographics, lists with items as well as charts. Handy, huh?

Mvelopes is available on both Android devices as well as iOS in addition to (BONUS) it's completely absolutely free. It is based on the envelope method for conserving money. With the envelope method, you take money out and split them into various envelopes, which are devoted to specific expenses (money entertainment, money etc.). Mvelopes allows you to perform this process digitally. Create a custom budget based on your expenditure and savings objectives. You can then add your various categories (bills and savings as well as debt repayment, cash entertainment, etc.). The program will record online transactions , or you can manually enter cash transactions into the app. Free version (yes there's also a paid version) provides up to 25 virtual envelopes.

Wally is a no-cost app that's available for Android as well as iOS. You can set an savings goal, create an expenditure budget and enter your income. These numbers are accessible on the main page so you can refer to them easily. It's simple to make and access all that data. It also offers a second layer of information as it comes with a location and socialization tool to allow you to analyze the amount you spend on what, where and how much money, and with whom you're spending time with when you are spending that money. In this way, you will find out if you have different or better spending habits when shopping with certain people, or shop at specific stores. It's useful and sure, it's an eye opener.

Spendbook It is an iOS application that costs around $2. It provides clients and users with a simple method to keep track of their expenditure. It is possible to add any the latest income or expenses quickly. It is possible to add a photograph of an item you recently purchased or a receipt must be classify. You can also sort your travel expenses via taxi, bus, or another. There's an overview option that allows you to see your daily expenses, as well as a monthly overview. You can also view graphs and infographics of your spending patterns.

The Level Money is a no-cost application that is accessible for both Android as well as iOS platforms. It's easy to use and extremely minimalist. It doesn't have a lot of whistles or bells however it is able to do the job. The app syncs with your accounts with financial institutions so that you are able to see the amount of money is to spend. It also displays the cost of your bills and asks you what percentage of of your earnings you would like to put into savings (then calculates it to you). After that, it displays how much you're able to invest in a tiny infographic.

If you'd like to get old school I've made a simple budget worksheet that you can complete below:

MONTHLY NET INCOME

The first income figure is $

The income #2 figure is $

Third Income $

Fourth Income $

Interest $

Other Costs

TOTAL REVENU $

Monthly FLEXIBLE EXPENSES

Food (indulgences) $

Entertainment Cost

Debt Payments in $

Other Dollars

Total FLEXIBLE EXPENSES $

Monthly fixed expenses

Mortgage/Rent/Housing $

Groceries Prices in $

Utilities $

Transportation Cost

Health Dollar

Other Costs

TOTAL FOLDED expenses $

TOTAL EXPENSES $

TOTAL MONTHLY REVENUE $

TOTAL EXPENSES MONTHLY $

Money left for savings

Monthly payments into Emergency Fund $

Total for Savings/Investments/Retirement Fund $

Other Dollars

Chapter 5: Understanding the Power In The Compound Effect

To to understand the significance of getting the compound effect to work for you, let's look at a few possible returns:

The Standard and Poor (S&P500) has, on a thirty year average, earned 11 percent. You can extend the 30-year period to 40, and the average is still 11 percent. Let's say you're 25 years old and you have set your sights on establishing your retirement plan now. If you went to the next step and set aside $1200 per year in the S&P 500 modelled index fund and the fund kept the 11 percent S&P 500 return:

The amount you would have earned was approximately $750,000 at the time that you reached pension age, which is 65.

If you decide to retire at the age of 55 the amount you would have earned in retirement, with the same contributions set it would be $265,000. If you decided to retire at the age of 45 the amount would be $80,000.

If, for any reason, you chose to die at age 35, you'd have saved around $22,000. The cost-to-income ratio of Index funds are low, around 20 basis points/0.20 percent or less. However, it is important to factor it in spite of its minor impact on the larger plan of the things.

The information above will provide a glimpse of the way compounding interest operates and the reason why the amount of time that it takes to complete is vital when it comes to the way it affects your finances. The image painted is an appealing one. However, the author will give you the complete picture without glossing over any details which is why this book:

Although you can say that the S&P 500 has given average returns of 11% over the last 40 years or but it hasn't performed as well lately. In the last two decades the average was close to 9 percent. In the past decade it has averaged 77 percent. Of of course, when we utilize round numbers, such as 11 percent or 9%, it's for the purpose of illustration. There are decimal numbers in addition to these round numbers.

Let's choose an amount of return which is more in line with the average of the past few years. 8percent is a good number. If we apply the same $1,200 contribution we'll get the following outcomes:

In the course of 40 years, you'll have amassed 3355,000

In the course of 30 years, you'll have earned 146,000

Over the course of 20 years you'll have earned $59,000

Over the course of 10 years you'll have earned $18,000

The numbers above might be lower than the prior ones, however they convey the same story as effectively. You are aware that the compounding effect is unavoidable and the numbers do not conceal anything. But, what's the primary takeaway you get when you examine the sums of the totals, with the 10-year spells separated by each?

The conclusion is that time is crucial. The person who begins the earliest will end with the most money. In the case of the last instance, the person who starts saving when he is 25 and then retires at age 65 will have more than twice the amount of money saved, as contrasted with the person who saves at age 35. This assumes the same amount of money saved each year.

In order to ensure that you have enough funds to invest in order to reap the benefits of the cumulative effect look at the most effective strategies you can use to gain more financial control and save even more.

Chapter 6: Building A Budget

Making the budget can be daunting initially however this chapter will guide you through each step of the entire process in order to create a smooth process.

1.Why Do You Want to Set Up A Budget?

Budget-conscious people are nearly twice as likely to experience financial anxiety contrasted to those who are spending and are less likely to go from paycheck to wage or have trouble managing financial issues.

While budgeting can be a beneficial method for everyone however, it is crucial to establish your goals prior to beginning the process, as the reason you've taken the decision to budget may determine the choices that you make while preparing your budget.

Although thinking about your motivations might seem like a waste of time, the psychology plays a major role in how you choose to manage your money. We will discuss the process of setting goals for budgeting since it is said earlier that If you've set some goals, it is more likely to adhere to your budget as you know what you're trying to achieve.

Setting Financial Goals

Being able to budget effectively means being able to establish financial goals and using your budget as an instrument to assist you in to achieve your objectives. You can set small goals like saving enough funds within a couple of months to purchase tickets for an event or movie, or more ambitious goals like making enough money to retire at age 50. You may even have multiple goals you're striving to achieve.

Other motives for coming up with a budget might be:

Reduce or eliminate the burden of

Don't spend cash you don't have

Breaking the cycle of wage to wages

Making sure you that the spending choices are in line with your values and your goals

Averting financial disputes between couples

Reduce spending on areas of concern

Becoming on track to meet the long-term and short-term financial goals

To reduce your expenses

A well-planned budget will allow you to define your long and short-term goals, and monitor your progress. This will allow these goals to be achieved.

When setting financial goals, it's crucial to stick to what is known as the SMART acronym. Let's take a look at this in more detail.

Specific: You must be precise regarding your financial goals and what you expect the budget will achieve. For example, instead of declaring, "I want to a budget that will help me end my overspending,"" make sure you have a specific motive, such as "I need a budget in order to make it easier to cut back on clothes and to only spend an amount." If you're looking to save money then you could set an objective like "I would like to in saving X quantity each month." Make sure that the goals you set are as precise as you can in order to can be sure of what you're striving for.

Measurable: How can you determine if you've achieved your objectives if you cannot determine their success. Make sure that no matter what goals you decide to set you are able to measure your performance to determine if you're moving in the right direction , or not.

Attainable Goals that can be achieved: The financial goals you establish must be attainable to allow you to think of strategies to reach your goals. Otherwise, you'll be disappointed by things you can't achieve. While the goal must be doable, it should be challenging enough to make you step outside from your comfortable zone, and test your boundaries.

Relevant: You should conduct a lot of soul-searching to ensure you've set goals that are relevant to you and that align with your values and goals otherwise, you'll be setting goals just in order to please other people or to be relevant but regret in the future that it was not what you really want.

The goals you set should be accompanied by time-bound goals. It's not enough to simply create a goal and then have the time frame you have set you will be able to reach your target. This is why having both long and short-term financial goals can be helpful.

Financial goals for the short term Goals for the short-term is one that you'd like to accomplish within less than 2 years. The goal is to put financial affairs in check by clearing credit card debt as well as making an emergency savings account. Other goals in the short-term financial realm might be to make small home improvements, purchasing new appliances for your home and saving money for a down payment on a car and so on.

Financial goals for the long-term include goals you'd like to accomplish within five years or less. These goals require you to implement a systematic strategy (effective spending) to reach them. One of the most common long-term financial goals of most people is to save enough money for retirement comfortably. Other financial goals that you might consider include paying off your student loan or mortgage off and traveling around the world, among others.

Financial goals that are long-term in nature are often a challenge because the future seems so far off. To ensure that you are on the right path, utilize online calculators to determine what amount you should save to reach your objectives. An excellent instance is to use the online calculator for long-term savings. It allows you to enter your specific variables like your age, your estimated rate of return for your investment, and the amount that you've saved to figure out how much you must save each month in order to reach your long-term goal.

Be aware that certain calculators on the internet produce different results. So, test using a couple calculators to obtain an estimate of the amount you'll need to put aside. It is crucial to begin to consider the amount that you accumulate each month as a non-negotiable monthly expense. If you are absolutely required, alter other categories of spending in order to make room to accommodate the savings categories.

Alongside making use of online calculators, you could also opt for automatic savings. Sometimes, we're too busy and we don't think about the savings commitments that we've made. To ensure that this doesn't happen and you meet the financial targets you have set, you should set up automatic deductions to will be deposited in the correct savings accounts you've established.

2.Calculate Your Total Earnings

Budgeting should assist you in making the most of your earnings more effectively. It is the reason you should know the amount you earn each month. Include your income from every source. This should include wage income and all investment income or business income as well as child support. the money earned made from other side ventures.

If your income for the month is not predictable, think about making yourself a wage first. That is, choose an invariable amount to build your budget around to help you save any extra cash you earn. This figure can be based on the amount you typically earn during a down month (if you're trying to minimize the chance of spending too much while making a bigger buffer) or on what you usually make on an average.

3.Be Be Accurate About Your Budget

It is essential to know what your current spending habits are prior to coming up with a an appropriate budget. Your budget is nothing more than an idea list that isn't feasible. When you determine the place where your money will go is when you'll be able to tell if your budget is feasible. It is recommended to record your expenses for an entire month to get an accurate picture of all your expenses. There are three ways you can employ to keep track of your expenses:

Through the use of statements

Statements from credit and bank accounts can assist you in tracking how much you spend. But, this method may not yield very precise results as you may not be able to remember what the specific transaction was used for. However, going back through the last month's reports can get you to the beginning of your budget since it provides a broad picture which you can take as a base.

Utilization of mobile apps

A few innovative apps like PocketGuard, Dollarbird, and Mint can make it easier to track purchases because it connects your bank accounts with the credit card accounts you have. Be sure to connect all your accounts that you own to ensure that every purchase is tagged in a way that allows for a precise evaluation.

Note your expenditure in an accounting spreadsheet or notebook

The most effective method of the three. However it's slow to complete. When you make a purchase on something, write it on paper or record it into the form of a spreadsheet. It is important to note every expense immediately following the transaction , so that you don't forget the numbers. Also, don't throw away your receipts.

4.Don't forget about insurance

As you calculate your expenses for the month, make sure that you have insurance. Unexpected events and catastrophes are a part of life in general, and if you're not properly insured your financial assets face the possibility of being destroyed.

Insurance is designed to safeguard your life and the life of your family, to ensure you have an enclosing on your roof and to ensure you are able to earn a steady income. Insurance such as homeowners' insurance, life insurance insurance as well as disability insurance may assist in the above scenarios.

It's now your turn to choose which type of life insurance policy you'll need in accordance with your financial requirements.

5.Choose an appropriate budgeting system

The most effective method of budgeting will depend on the goals you want to accomplish. Are you looking to save money or reduce debt, or do you just want to limit your spending? All of the budgeting methods that we have learned about earlier are created to help you analyze and better understand your relationship to money. Although they might share an objective however, they typically employ different strategies to accomplish it. It's up to you to pick the one that is most suitable for you.

Here are some things to take into consideration when selecting the best budgeting strategy:

How long are you budgeting?

If this is the first time that you're looking to establish a budget then the 50/30/20 method is the one that is most appropriate or for you. The reason this approach is attractive for beginners is the fact that it divides your income into three main categories: necessities essentials, savings, and needs. It allows you to have plenty of space to settle your debt, pay for your current expenses, and also put aside money for your future. It can be used in conjunction with it or as a base to develop a budget that is suited to your needs.

Are you looking to get the most out of every cent

If you're a meticulous planner or who is prone to spending too much and overspend, Zero Based Budget will satisfy both your requirements. The strategy makes the process of budgeting and monitoring easy. Once you have earned your money it is essential to make use of every dollar in a systematic manner. This prevents excessive spending because every dollar is a part of.

You want to manage your spending

If you're just looking to avoid debt or cut down on the frequency of spending that isn't your priority, but you do not want to keep track of every penny you spend, then you'll require a firm system like the envelope system for budgeting. This approach allows you to establish a limit for each expense category including groceries and utilities and then fill the envelopes with the money you have allocated, and use the cash to pay to pay for the specific expenses. If the cash in a particular envelope is out, you'll not be able to make more purchases in that particular category until the next month and this can instill some form of financial discipline, especially if you've been spending a lot.

You'd like to accumulate some savings

If the sole purpose of budgeting is to accumulate savings then this Pay Yourself First strategy will help you reach that target. This method of budgeting is created to align your priorities and your spending habits, so it is not surprising that it puts savings first over other expenses that are immediate. When you receive your pay the system lets you determine how much you'd like to reserve to fund goals like an emergency savings account or retirement. The rest you can make use of for other expenses such as charges.

6.Have A Household Reunion

If you're with a friend make sure they are on board because budgeting is a group project. However, if you're a single, there is no need to think about it. Engaging your significant other is essential since, as per an investigation conducted of SunTrust Bank, 35% of those who were in a partnership or relationship thought it was money that caused the primary reason for conflict in their relationship.

While you're having the discussion about money, you should make it simple your partner to be involved in the discussion in a meaningful way. Start with the basics of a budget, which include costs like utility bills, food items and gas. Then , you can consider the ways you make use of your extra money for things such as eating out, shopping and other costs should be.

To make it even easier, think about breaking down your monthly earnings into weekly portions to help you manage your cash. In this way, when you've used up all your money to the point of exhaustion, both must stop spending. As the close of the month draws near review your budget and compare it to how you used the money. This strategy, especially if the two of you have been involved in budgeting, can take some stress on your loved ones and to avoid arguments that might be a result of every expense.

7.Keep All Tracks of Every Cost Whatever the amount

After you've settled on the budgeting approach you will apply, how can you begin to implement it? Certain payments, like rent or mortgages are simple to keep track of. But for other costs, you'll have to keep receipts. If you think that's too time-consuming, you can keep track of all your expenses using the same debit and credit card to make the process of recording simple. It is crucial to keep in mind that the descriptions of transactions that appear on the credit card statement may not always be transparent, and could make you wonder what this $20.13 purchase is.

Alternately, you can utilize physical cash for incidental expenses. Be sure to have money in your account by withdrawing the exact amount each week or on a monthly basis. You can categorize this as'miscellaneous. This method could help you avoid spending too much however it may not give the most clear picture yet of where your money is going.

Here are some suggestions to help you keep track of your expenditures:

Update your budget every day

Monitoring your cash every day is quick and easy and also makes sure that you do not forget the cost of any purchase.

Use precise descriptions

Write down the expenses you incur in writing. Write down the reason the location where you purchased them. This way, you'll informed of the amount you spend on a particular area. For example, if you go out to eat in McDonald's or Starbucks or other places, you could create orders that include coke or iced coffee, burgers or salads. If you just record all your orders under McDonald's then you'll not be able to pinpoint where the money was spent.

8.Reward Yourself

When your financial plan is designed to generate savings solely for boring tasks like savings for unexpected expenses of medical bills or repair work on your vehicle or to pay off debt, the only motivation to save will be the uncertainty of what might happen the next time you do not. While fear is an effective motivator, in a state of fear is not a good idea for anyone.

Even when your debt is at the bottom of your pile and you're determined to pay it off as quickly as you can You could also make a difference by adding rewards to your savings plan.

However, it's essential to recognize yourself for the achievements you accomplish. Include reward systems in your budget for the month. For example, if you stick to the budget plan for just a few months, you can set aside money to go to a movie or dinner out together with your partner or a best friend. In the next few months, you can set aside cash for a getaway. By doing this you turn this budgeting procedure a contest that rewards yourself for demonstrating prudent financial behaviour.

The issue about budgeting is that it's not fixed in stone. it is crucial to recognize that things aren't working as you planned and adjust. We will discuss changing to your financial plan within the subsequent chapter.

Chapter 7: Basics of Budgeting

No matter what method you employ to budget it is essential to grasp the fundamental concepts that you must apply. These tools and concepts are crucial to the success of your budget. It is essential to use them with care especially when you're just beginning your journey. It is essential to utilize the information gathered from these tools to assist you in develop a budget that is accurate and effective.

The tracking of income

There are several important points to be aware of when tracking your income. It is important for your budget to be as accurate as you can. If you are overestimating the amount of income you'll have, it could cause your whole budget out of balance. It's possible that you'll be short in the entire month or week and not be able to pay a major expense.

When you look at your income to budget you must consider every source of income that is reliable. This means you have to include only those incomes that are guaranteeable. This will usually be your pay. If you are calculating the amount you'll receive you will need, don't consider your gross earnings. If you're working the same amount of hours per week, you could take the net earnings from your pay stubs to determine the amount you can plan for your income. If you work in different hours then calculate your gross income and subtract 25% for tax. There may be fewer deductions however it's safer to be cautious instead of not be.

You could also have additional sources of revenue, such as those from an extra job or child support, or Alimony. If you are able to earn regular income from any of these sources, which is guaranteed, you are welcome to include it into your income budget. Guaranteed income is the income that is paid on a regular basis. It is also required to be received in a continuous manner and at the same time every day for at least three or six months.

If you're in possession of an alimony or child support order , but the money doesn't always arrive on time or in any form and you don't want to consider it income when you budget. If you plan for this amount and the money doesn't come in, it could throw your whole financial plan off track and you could confront potentially severe consequences.

The process of tracking expenses

There are a variety of ways you can monitor your spending and expenses. It is particularly important to track expenses as you begin budgeting. It is crucial to be aware of where your money goes. Setting up a budget that outlines the things you expect to spend money on is a crucial part in your spending plan. The way you track expenses can tell you how much money you're actually going.

The importance of tracking expenses is that it lets you know what you have to plan for. Rent and car loan are fixed costs which you don't need to think about. However, the majority of expenses are variable, which means that they vary every month. It is the only method to plan variable costs is to have an idea of what the amount could be.

It's fairly easy to keep track of your expenses. You can make a spreadsheet using your personal computer, where you add your expenses each day and keep a monthly total that you can view at the lower end of the. There are spreadsheets of this type accessible online too. This involves keeping receipts and logging every expense.

It is also possible to get expense tracking devices on your mobile smartphone with a range of applications. This can be helpful in making sure you don't overlook any expense when you input them into your expense tracking system at home. If you're a single person, you may utilize the app to track expenses. If you are married, you'll need to integrate your expenses and theirs onto an excel spreadsheet or other software.

Budgeting for variable expenses

Here is the place where an expense tracking device can be useful. When you record your expenditure during the month prior, you can use the information to budget those expenses that are variable for the next month. If you keep this pattern going, you can estimate the average cost for each item, based on a few months of information. This will provide you with the most accurate budget that you can possibly get.

It is crucial to allow yourself some flexibility in the case of variables in your costs. Always make sure to reduce them, even by a couple of dollars in the course of calculating your budget. This will ensure that you do not have to worry about a problem when the amount may end up being larger than you expected. If you've got extra money at the end of your budget due to padding your variable expenses, you can make use of it to buy more expensive items which you were unable to afford prior or you can save it in your savings fund.

It is recommended to budget as precisely as is possible. Like we said, your expense tracker can assist you in some ways. Your past expenditure habits can help determine your budget for items like food, gas and household goods. Some variable expenses require a different tactic.

If you are paying utility bills like it is important to review your previous charges for this year. That is If it's summer it is important to go back to see what your average cost was for the summer before. This is usually done by contacting your utility provider and asking for the data. If this is the first time living in your home you may still call the utility company. They will provide you with the estimates of utility charges for the month of the previous year, based on the usage of previous residents.

Tips for Budgeting Your Grocery

Budgeting for groceries can be one of the most difficult variables costs to estimate. The cost of food varies widely. There are times when you can find incredible deals and get amazing sales, but at other times you'll have to pay all price regardless of where in the city to shop. The prices of meat can fluctuate. Many things could alter the cost of food in a matter of minutes or little notice.

Your previous expenditure will give you a reference place for your grocery budget. Review a few months of expenses to determine the amount you'll spend on average. You should try to pick the more expensive number in order to ensure you are budgeted enough.

It is also helpful to create an eating plan for your budget create a shopping list and calculate the amount you'll spend to complete the list. It is also advisable to increase your budget to ensure that you're able to afford grocery items in the event of price increases or something unexpected happens.

There's a fantastic tool you can make use of to help improve your grocery budget. precise. You can create an excel spreadsheet for it. There are a number of websites and apps that can assist you in this. It is essential to keep track of each item you purchase. Bring the receipt from your grocery store and enter the store's date and time, item, size and cost. This way, you'll be able to determine exactly what you have paid for every item.

When you have your meal plan for the upcoming budget period , you can look back over your list of items and determine the amount you paid on each of the items. Your shopping list will be completed and you'll have the exact amount of what you'll spend. Most people don't have the time however if you are able, this is an excellent instrument that can be very helpful to you.

Chapter 8: Budgeting To Your Goals

Every financial goal is different. You must take an approach to achieving each goal based on the amount you require and the amount of time you have left for saving.

In the pursuit of short-term financial goals

In your list of financial commitments, it is important to categorize each item based on whether they are short-term or long-term ones.

In budgeting, the term "short-term" refers to financial obligations have to be paid in the next calendar year. One example of a brief-term financial obligation is your bills. There are bills that you have to pay each month. For instance, let's say that your electricity service provider typically costs the equivalent of $100 per month. You paid the last month's usage. The next payment is due within one month. You will have around sixty days to save up for the next $100 installment. If you receive your paycheck twice each month, you will have two chances to save your electric bill.

A childish budgeter may overlook it on the first payday , and pay for the entire amount on the next payday. This can cause an enormous amount of stress on the budgeter as the payment date is near.

A budgeter who is financially stable will save a money to pay for electricity. He will save $100 every month, with $50 each payday. When the utility bill is lower than $100, he'll put the remaining amount into the electricity fund. This will be used later on when the bill for electricity is higher than normal.

You can handle all of your short-term expenses similarly. Below are some steps you must follow when saving for short-term goals

You must determine the amount you require.

After that, you must determine the amount of time you've got to save. You can then calculate the amount of paydays that between now and your goal date. If you earn other forms that are regular in your income make sure to add them to the total.

Then, you should divide the amount you require by the amount of paydays.

If you are required to pay $1000 over 8 months that's 16 paydays from now until the date of your goal. This assumes you receive your pay bi-monthly. If you follow the procedure above, it means that you will only need to save 63 bucks each month to achieve your target. If you do this in this manner it makes saving more manageable. Without this approach, the majority of people will only begin saving once the deadline was close. This, as mentioned earlier, can be stressful.

Saving for the long-term goal

The long-term financial goals are more difficult. These are financial commitments that you have to take on for in the next year or more the present. The issue with long-term objectives is that they typically require a substantial amount. Saving up for a home, for instance, is a long-term target. The huge sums required for these objectives usually scare financially inexperienced individuals.

Do not let the size of the money to deter you. Long-term goals can be challenging but they can be accomplished. To learn how to save money for your personal long-term goals The steps you must do:

Determine the experience or item you're saving up for and what amount you will need. Understanding what you're working for will inspire you to put in the effort and make savings. If you truly desire something, you'll be able to justify the sacrifices you have to make.

Learn about how others have achieved similar goals. If you're planning to save to build a home, for instance it is important to know the specifics of building the home in your local area. You must consider where you can get the required resources and workforce to construct that dream house. It is also important to know about the financing solutions that are that can help you achieve your goals.

If you're planning to build an apartment, you have to be aware of the different kinds of loans for housing that are available to you. Cash payments are always the most economical choice. If you already have a house to live in at the moment it is possible to make savings for your home in order to avoid higher interest charges of mortgages for housing.

One of the best ways to get information about this is to talk with those who have accomplished similar results. It is advisable to search your contacts for those who recently constructed or purchased an apartment. It is then advisable to call them to obtain the information you require. It is recommended to plan your questions prior to the time to ensure you don't overlook any information.

Choose the most economical payment method for you

In our case it is possible to save up for a house when you allow yourself the time to save, and you will be able to avoid costly rent charges. Some people find that the option of a home loan can be less expensive in the event that they consider the amount they will have to pay for rent over the time they're saving.

It is important to think about the various options to accomplish the long-term objectives you have set. It is important to research how other people have achieved their goals. After studying the ways other people have reached similar goals, it is important to select the most affordable method to you, but without getting rid of quality.

Be patient, but save slowly

Like with short-term objectives it is essential to save money for your long-term goals every payday. Since you are saving an amount that is substantial it is important to make sure you save as much as you can every payday by using the budgeting strategies in the earlier chapters.

Make your money difficult to access

Since it takes a long time to achieve your goal, you might be tempted to pull out the cash and use it to fund another purpose. To prevent this from happening you must put the funds in money accounts which are challenging to access.

If you have goals that must be accomplished within the next two years, such as, for example, you could place the money into an account at a bank that does not have an ATM card. To withdraw the funds it is necessary to visit the bank and request it from the bank teller.

Make sure you invest your money in your most important ambitions

A few of the largest objectives require between 7 and 20 years to attain. Saving for your child's college savings, for instance is a long period of time. It's not advisable to let these kinds of funds sit idle. It is essential to put these funds in investment vehicles that are low risk. This will allow the funds to keep pace with inflation during the savings time. In addition to the time invested this money will increase over time and you could be able to achieve your goals quicker.

Chapter 9: Easy Strategies to Help Your Budget Work for You

Make a list of expenses

When I say you have expenses, I'm talking about all of them , including your tiny ones like the ones discussed earlier. Certain of the larger expenses such as your rent are simple since you are able to recall them. It's easy to forget about the smaller costs. To ensure you are aware of these expenses, you should ensure that you save the receipts to record or make a recording following the purchase of the day. Another method is to place them under miscellaneous items. This will provide you with the complete overview of what's happening with your financials. It is possible to use the envelope technique to make the process process easier for you. If you prefer to pay online, you could be placing all the money you have to spend on every item you purchase into an account that is operating or a debit card. Then, you can make payments using that card only. It is easy to look over the statements and find out what you bought when and from where.

Update your budget daily

This is to help you not lose track of small purchases. You can utilize Evernote to track your expenses at the time you make them. This ensures that there isn't a huge time gap between the time you made the purchase and the time you write it down. Utilize cloud storage solutions such as Dropbox to allow you to make changes to your document at any time and anywhere you'd like.

Use a complete description

Instead of listing the place where you went shopping rather, you should be listing the specific items you purchased at the store. It's easy to summarize the purchase by categorizing them into categories like grocery items, clothing or household cleaning items.

Budget according to month and not by paycheck

We all earn at various dates, so instead planning your budget based on when your pay check arrives it is better making your budgets on an annual basis. This will give you a more long time frame and also the possibility of starting from scratch each month. This also means the event of an unlucky month the month will end and become a memory.

Plan for occasional expenses

It is a good idea to set aside some funds for various events that can occur throughout the year particularly in the case of a the strictest budget. You could decide to classify them under the category of miscellaneous. Incorrect pay can cause the budget to be difficult to manage. But, it's feasibleto attempt to calculate your minimum wage and base your budget on it. If you have any extra money then you can set it aside for bad days.

You may face problems with Your Budget if:

It's more complicated than it has to be

It is not reflective of your values. This happens especially when you decide to duplicate someone else's budget.

It is not reflective of the real world; it must be based on your actual earnings and expenses should be in line with the expenses you actually have and not the ones you believe you have incurred.

It's like a chore, but make budgeting fun , because that's the purpose of it in your life. To make you enjoy life!

It's not feasible Remember we discussed using your SMART acronym when you set your budget and goals? Revisit that, and things will become easier.

Be flexible

Don't feel confined to staying within your budget. It is possible to pay more during a specific month because of guests, so allow yourself to. But make sure to take a cut from a different expense you are able to cut out to pay for it.

Have a blast!

You must ensure that there is enough money in your budget for some fun. It all depends on the amount of money you have available. You don't have to be spending a lot of money on yourself. Let your budget be able to allocate some funds for things you could do to reward yourself. This is the only motivation you can get to help you work harder. If your budget doesn't permit this, then it can be difficult to stick to it.

Do not make more than you earn

Spend less the money you're earning. It is a fact that there will be holiday seasons every year. As opposed to waiting for the moment to spend on large purchases, you could be purchasing gifts all year.

Do not take on debts you don't need.

If you are not sure that something is an investment that will last for a long time it is not a reason to take on the debt market because of it. You should be able to recognize the investments you can make, such as a home or education. When you purchase something like an automobile, be aware that the value decreases each year. This isn't something you would want to enter into debt to purchase.

Saving and Budgeting = Happiness and Less Worry

It is not enough to talk about budgeting and not discuss the savings. The main purpose of budgeting is to ensure you have enough cash for the event of a rainy day rather than living pay check to paycheck. How do you ensure that you adhere to your savings plan as stipulated in the rules for budgeting previously mentioned? How can you transform your lifestyle to save each month? Let's look at some options:

Make sure you pay yourself first.

The most efficient method of saving money is to ensure that you don't get hold of it initially. You could open a savings bank account and then make arrangements with your bank to transfer the money directly to your other account. I mentioned direct deposit in the past. The only money accessible is the money that you can use.

Beware of accumulating new credit

Do your best not to fall into debt, or at the very least not every day. Most of us aren't in a position to buy items without incurring debt. We're just hooked on credit card debt! But, remember that the longer it takes to settle your debts, the higher interest you pay and the more you'll need to pay over the long term.

Set reasonable goals for savings

It is simpler to save if you know what you're saving for. Set a goal for what you would like to achieve and then set aside funds for it. Did you notice how much easier you can save to pay for an event like a wedding? Even if you have to take on financial obligations, you're being pressured to make sure you raise the most feasible! Simply decide what you would like to invest in and decide how much you'd like to spend on this.

Set a timeframe to achieve your goals.

You should set reasonable saving time limitations. Set them high, but make them doable. Attaining each goal is often an motivator. If you're in the middle of a time when you'll know exactly the amount you'll need to dedicate to saving to realize your goals.

Begin saving as early as you can

The longer your money sits at the banks, the sooner it begins earning interest rates. It is crucial to begin saving as soon possible. This is even with the lowest amount of money you are able to afford.

You might want to consider making a contribution to an account for retirement

You'd like to enjoy a comfortable retirement. The only way to achieve this is when you begin making contributions into your retirement. Remember that retirement funds typically have restrictions that could stop you from accumulating the funds you've been saving. It is simple to understand that, in retirement, you will only withdraw it when you are forced to do so. This is a good method of keeping your cash free from your endless need to spend.

Don't be discouraged.

The process of saving can be a challenging process, especially if you're facing financial difficulties. Be positive at every stage of your journey. It's going to improve and become easier. Once you've started be aware of the cost.

While you are saving it is important to accept the fact that your costs aren't going to stop demanding your attention. Here are some suggestions and strategies to aid you in cutting costs to save money:

Eliminating expenses

Cut out the luxuries in your budget

In our previous discussion about budgeting, we mentioned that having amusement is healthy. It helps break up the monotony and allows you to take pleasure in the money you earn. It doesn't mean that your budget must be filled with extravagant items; the amount you spend should be reduced to a minimum.

Find a cheaper rental

Find a cheaper house in a secure neighborhood. This will allow you put the money you're earning to other activities.

This could be used to save for retirement, or the house you want to buy.

Stay clear of expensive addictions

Addictions are among the negative habits that prevent you from saving. A few of these are smoking, drinking, and engaging in other forms of substances. Be aware of the harmful impacts they have on your health and your wallet.

Be healthy and stay fit

Hospital expenses can wipe out your savings in an extremely short period of period of time. This is something you don't want to occur. So, pay attention to your diet and do your best to remain healthy. This keeps your money and budget in check! Additionally, you should contribute to a medical insurance plan. While you may argue that you don't have to be sick every day If there is a chance, you earnings is reduced (you can't work when suffer from illness) while your money savings will also be wiped out by medical bills.

Chapter 10: Tips to be financially smart

Women, with their knowledge, will be the foundation for you to be the most effective financial manager. Being a traditional homemaker , with no knowledge of financial matters is only going to make things more difficult for you, and your progress will be stagnant. We're not trying to be the underdogs of the circumstances in this instance. The majority of housewives manage the expenses that are paid monthly on their behalf by spouses. They don't have an interest in the way that money flow is being handled and the way in which their house is being taken care of. The husbands are the ones who manage investments and other financial related matters.However emergencies can come knocking on at any time without notice.

A friend with me Paula made the decision to go for it two years ago. A stay-at-home mom and the person in charge of her household financial plan, Paula had a clear plan to manage the whole financial aspect in a parallel fashion with her partner. An investment that was not made according to recommendations from their manager led to a massive loss of $2000 to the family. It was an alarm for her. Maybe a bit of vigilance and knowledge of the investment could have prevented the loss. In just 6 months of her loss, she reformed herself into an expert in the field of finance.

Following the massive loss she had to face, she took a deep breath herself and decided that her understanding of finance will go far beyond paying her husband's salary. It was also imperative to approach the issue with more care. The first step was to sign up in an online finance course. It helped her understand the fundamentals of finance includes understanding of investing as well as taxation, banking along with insurance, debit, credit system , etc. Within a short time, Paula grasped the crux of everything.

Alongside this she also changed her love for novels with more finance-related books. The book racks are now well organized and she offers homemakers a book. Reading does not have a limit. She grew wings and learned from personal finance magazines as well as economic papers.

The way she watched television was changed also. She stopped engaging with entertainment channels, and instead moved to commercial channels. In addition, she spoke to an independent financial adviser who was later her guide and an important way to reach higher levels. Based on the suggestions from her advisor, she attended a variety of seminars and workshops in the city.

Paula is now more conscious and alert. She keeps an eye on all the financial aspects of her household's budget, investments , and securities. She is aware of the fact that the conditions of the economy, share markets policy, investment climate and the policies remain in flux. There will be sunny days and cloudy days. If one wishes to safeguard their future and keep enough money to meet requirements of the day you must act at the right time.

Opportunities are fleeting; smart people are the ones who gets the most of it. The quarterly or weekly business news releases, while keeping you updated on the latest developments can also help you get a thorough understanding of financial matters, learn the opinions by financial specialists, offer you reviews and compare different products, provide you with the latest information on real estate information and inform you about the biggest players on the market. If you keep up with them, you will get an idea of the baskets to place your eggs in . That is where you can make a better investment to reap higher returns.

Along with everything else, the internet is the central repository of all information. If it is used in a proper method, it can be the best resource to study everything from the basic to the higher financial levels. A well-rounded knowledge base can safeguard you from scams and frauds. You'll become more aware and more able to distinguish between investments that are good and those that are not. Additionally, you can ensure that all of your tax, insurance, loans and credit are taken care of carefully. This gives you the confidence of being secure , but also lets you make a better life for your family and you.

Do not undervalue your capabilities and capabilities. Whatever the subject may appear to be to you It's only an issue of taking that first step. It is important to be aware of the value of knowledge particularly in financial matters. It's your ideal companion to guide through the financial storm. It's never too late to master the art of financial planning and, at the end of the day, you'll be able to stand tall as a wise woman. Paula isn't a superwoman. She is in me, in you and every woman who is the house manager. her house.

Financial status, education age, learning skills, and financial status are not important. All that is important is perseverance and honesty. We're not trying to become a professional financial planner but rather to be prudent and wise. Start small and eventually you'll be there Paula is now!

Chapter 11: The Advantages of Budgeting

Controlling Yourself

One of the advantages of having budgets is that you will be able to know how much you are spending each week or month. By knowing this, you'll better manage your finances , and easily determine if you have things that need to be taken care of.

A budget will allow you to adjust your financial plan to any changes resulting from unexpected circumstances. If you have an emergency or unexpected increases to the cost of your bills each month, you'll not be stressed because you're prepared for such scenarios.

Budgeting lets you have control over your finances instead of letting money control you. It lets you determine what you wish for it. Being in control lets you determine whether you should save money, invest it or invest it to get rid of debt.

A budget can alter your perspective toward money and assist you in establishing the proper way of using it. Instead of spending cash in recklessly, you'll be able to utilize it to satisfy your requirements and achieve the financial targets you have set. You will learn to manage and control yourself so that you can become more accountable in financial issues.

Clear Monitor

Another benefit when you budget is you'll be aware of the exact location of your money. Budgeting is a useful self-education tool which will reveal how much you earn and where it goes and how much is left after you have paid every expense. A budget can prevent you from being shocked when you realize that the income is declining. Knowing how to manage your expenditure will allow you to plan better for the future and will help you to be prepared for any emergency.

A budget that is detailed will assist you in monitoring your unwise ways of spending money. It will also help you discover the root of the waste and take steps to fix the problem.

By budgeting, you'll not be able to think each month where you have spent your money. It lets you determine what you are able to spend your money on in relation to your financial standing. It provides you with an accurate picture of your priorities, based on the way you spend your money and how it benefits you. It also allows you to have an overall overview of your financial situation. If you keep a budget in place it is possible to avoid having an obligation.

A financial monitor can help in making sure that the amount money that goes out is lower than what is coming into. If you don't have this, you could overspend more than you can afford, which could result in you becoming debt-ridden. It's easy to lose track of your finances if you don't have an account of your budget because you aren't able to monitor the amount of money that comes in and goes.

Opportunities

If you don't adhere to a set budget, you may not have enough money to fund other options like saving up for the purchase of a car, the house you want, or the start of a new business. Budgeting lets you save money for other reasons like vacation or gifts for celebrations.

With a budget plan it is possible to set goals and achieved, such as creating a house, setting up an enterprise, or funding college tuition for every child. Because budgeting can help you save money, you'll have the funds to achieve the objectives.

Good Organization

With budgeting, you'll be more organized as it allows you to build the ability to manage your personal financial situation, your income as well as savings and expenditures. If you have expenses that exceed the income you earn, you may adjust your spending during the next few months or even months to regulate your financial flow.

The creation of a budget will force the family to stay within the budget of their monthly income. Families will become aware of their budget and be more cautious not to overspend.

When you divide your money into categories , such as savings and expenses, a plan will help you understand the way each category uses a portion from your money.A budget also serves as a way to organize the financial statement and bill. By organising every financial transaction, you'll be able to cut down on time and energy.

Better Communication

The subject of finances and money are among the most frequent causes of disputes between couples. The majority of the time, disagreements arise due to a lack of planning and organization regarding financial issues. A budget plan can assist you communicate better with your spouse or other family members. It allows you to share your thoughts and discuss the strategy of how you will make use of the funds with family members.

A budget for the family can help you discuss your goals, financial challenges, and plans with your fellow members. Discussions with your family about the budget will also let you to understand the distinct priorities of each person that will allow you to deal with these issues effectively.

This also helps to foster the bonding between family members and helps avoid conflicts in the topic of the way money is spent. Budgeting can also help everyone in the family to be more accountable and responsible in the way they spend money. It helps build trust within the family also build a sense of unity.

Reduce worries

A budget can help you to prepare for coming emergencies. The ability to keep track of your financial position will help you recognize the possible financial challenges that may arise in the future. You'll be able to alter your financial plan before issues arise.

If you have a budget in place it will be easier to know the amount of debt you can handle without concerned about not having enough. It is possible to avoid the burden of debt after having developed and maintained a successful budget.

Savings

A budget plan can provide various ways to reduce the cost from your monthly earnings to serve various needs. A budget can assist you to control your finances and help you save to meet your long-term and short-term goals. If you're more mindful when it comes to your finances, you'll be able to make saving the top of your list.

Additionally, budgeting lets you to plan and set aside funds for the event of an emergency. When an unexpected requirement arises you can draw from your savings for emergencies. Also, you will learn to control your costs and reduce unnecessary expenses such as fees, interest and penalties.

Budgeting clearly shows you how to manage your money in accordance with your financial limits. It prevents you from spending too much and accumulating debt. If you make savings your priority and savings, you'll be able to reduce your spending habits, and you will learn to manage your money effectively.

Chapter 12: What to Travel on a Budget

Traveling has always been a subject of an expensive price. However, over the past few years, we've heard stories of people from all over the globe who travel with small budgets and simply determination - like the couple who went between Bulgaria to India through hitchhiking! Of course, you'll not choose to pursue this as a full-time occupation, but it's very easy to travel on an income-based budget.

There are many helpful websites and blogs online that provide tips about how to travel with an affordable budget, which places are the most ideal to stay, what attractions worth visiting, and so on and so on; each offering photos to back up their claims! This can all be completed at your home or in the comfort of your chair at your home.

In this article we will examine ways to get the most value from your budget-friendly holiday!

1. Learn about bargains on coach, air trains, ships, or ferry tickets on the web. There are many companies that provide a great method to accomplish this. Make sure you get the greatest advantage of low-cost transporters - rail, air and coach. They typically offer lower rates for destinations that are common to traditional carriers at a cost which is lower or half of the cost of.

It is possible to use Amtrak to travel by rail within America. U.S., for Europe you could consider Eurail for non-EU residents as well as Interrail specifically for EU citizens. Both of them offer tickets to international trains.

Coaches can be used to travel between cities after you have reached the destination. Greyhound is available in America and Eurolines in Europe. U.S along with Eurolines in Europe provide discounts in coach ticket prices. Certain travel routes are cross-country, so find out the options that are provided. Megabus also is a European company that provides travel to more than forty-five European countries, as well as routes that travel on northwestern North American continent.

Utilize websites like sky scanner or kayak, or even travel store to discover cheap options to fly. These sites provide comparison information regarding flight tickets, and can aid you in finding the most affordable ticket. Hosting sites for Mediator like Travelocity and Opodo offer discounts on tickets as well as trips to airports.

If you are planning to travel by vessel or cruise, it could be a bargain in the event that you can get food and accommodation included in the cost. There are companies like Star cruises , and Cunard which offer transatlantic travel. There are websites like The Cruise People which can compare the prices of cruises for you.

Hack: Make sure you clean your cookies each when you look for tickets or prices. Browsers store these bits of data and websites make use of them to increase the price up each time you visit the site to look for alternatives and other possibilities. Once you've made a decision on the best option, clear your browser's history, remove the cookies and launch the site. You'll be amazed by the difference in price!

2. In the case of accommodations on the internet, it's your best friend. Look up information on the internet and find a list of the hostels for backpackers and youth hostels that you can locate in the area you're looking to go to. Remember, you simply require a place to stay. This doesn't mean it needs to be a top of the line.

It is also possible to travel via sleeper trains in order to cover the distance between destinations and also get a night's sleep, too!

Hack Hack: Hack: The YMCA is found in every city. Hostels like these offer an affordable option for stay. Be aware that when you take vacation, you'll be spending the majority of your day traveling. It's not sensible to pay a large sum for an accommodation that you only use for a few hours and that's not even getting only a couple of hours of rest in.

3. If you have family members who live in the area you would like to visit, inquire with them to see if you can live with them and save money on expenses for living. Be sure to adhere to the rule of three days which means you need to ensure that you don't outstay your stay.

Be a nice host, and ensure that your home is neat and tidy. Make your bed every morning before you get up, and help by doing the chores.

Hack: Make use of websites, such as Travelsherpa and other, which provide local residents with the opportunity to host tourists. The world is opening and you can reside with locals. Be aware of the three-day rule. And of course remember to give your host a rating. Do it to show your love!

4. You can save money by walking around. It's a Lot! Go to free or cheap attractions, and take advantage of inexpensive public transportation or shuttle buses. It is possible to learn more about a city walking around on foot as well as spending less on transportation.

Meet with locals and visitors who seem friendly. This is your most reliable source for knowing more about the things to do and to stay clear of. Ask travel guides about how to spend more time without spending much.

Check for details online prior to you go to a location so you can find the best price for your money.

Hack: Many centers of entertainment or tourist attractions have discounts for booking in advance. When you've selected a destination look up the attractions on Google and find discounts for booking in advance. It will eliminate the hassle of waiting in lines and is cheaper than making tickets reservations on the same day or even the week before your scheduled trip.

5. One thing you should be aware of when traveling is to pack the food you would normally consume. Bring soup and noodles, so you are able to travel for a lengthy time and only spend a tiny amount of money. Be aware that you're in the country for the adventure not for first-class eating. If you don't have soup packs, try local restaurants that offer meals for less and have the added benefit of getting to know the local culture, and eating lots of tasty food.

Photograph a lot to create memories, make a travel journal that puts smiles on your face each time you browse through it!

Hack: Take sachets of creamer and coffee, and several biscuit packets. Many hotels provide a kettle as well as pure drinking water. It doesn't require much effort or expense to get an enjoyable cup of coffee! The kettle can be used to make instant noodles!

6. If you are booking your hotel online, reserve it for the night you'll be staying. So you'll have somewhere to stay when you arrive at your destination, and you won't need to think about finding another location. It's then possible to walk around on the next day to locate locations that are more suited for your financial budget. It is also possible to leave your luggage here without the need to move it around in search of the new location.

There's of course numerous other tricks and tips you can use when traveling to ensure you make the most of your trip, but not only the location. All you have to do is to learn more!

Hack: Search for websites like AirBnB and Agoda in addition to TripAdvisor and many others that all offer the most affordable cost. Like with travel tickets be sure to clear the cookies in your browser, then reopen the site and book your trip. It could take longer however it's worthwhile when you've got an extra $100-$200 to spend!

Chapter 13: Monitoring and Readjusting to Ensure Success

Although the strategies in the previous section are beneficial but they aren't easy to implement if you are facing many spending temptations in your life. To keep the items and happenings around you from impacting your budgeting performance it is essential to think about how to encourage yourself to stick to your budget plan.

Motivation to stick to the plan

Your budgeting approach should begin at the time you first wake to get up. If you lose your vigilance you might slip up and not follow some of the budgeting techniques that you are advised to achieve.

To avoid this being a reality, you need to keep a record of the reason you're trying in order to cut costs. If you're saving money to go on a trip for instance it is possible to put an image of your trip destination on your refrigerator and on your desk. You can place it in the same spot as the photos of your loved ones to remind yourself of the people you will be spending time with at these locations.

It is also possible to have a list of things that you are allowed to purchase and keep in your account. Anything that is not on the list shouldn't be bought or purchased. The discipline required to be an effective budgeter is quite high. You'll have to discover the right tools for motivation that match your individuality.

Additionally it is important to organize your schedule to be aware of what you'll accomplish at any given time. In preventing unexpected events occurring it will allow you to reduce your expenses. This will stop any unplanned costs.

Establish a budgeting system that supports budgeting.

It is also important to speak to people you communicate with often about your strategies.

When people decide to begin budgeting, they generally don't reveal to their family or friends about the process. They simply make excuses as to the reasons why they can't invest their cash. This can result in broken relationships and breaking up with their friends.

When you speak to people you regularly interact with You can explain what you're experiencing. The majority of people will be able to be able to understand the situation and not judge you if you decide to be cautious about spending.

If this occurs it is normal to reduce the activities that we do for fun. These are the kinds of activities we enjoy with buddies to unwind and get away from all the problems we have. These kinds of activities aren't required for survival however they are efficient in helping people connect and build stronger connections.

If you let the people who you typically spend time with understand why you're cutting back in your spending, you'll be able to keep your relationships , while adhering to your budget. You will be able to return in a more frequent relationship after you've reached your goals or when your earnings increase and you have more money to spend.

Inform your family members about the changes that have to be implemented.

In order to make your budgeting effective it is also necessary to discuss your budget with family members to ensure that they are prepared to handle the lifestyle and financial changes about to take place. If your kids have grown up with large allowances at school, you may have to cut back on the amount you pay to them. It is a difficult thing to accept for a majority of children. But, it could be necessary to take this step if you are trying to get there faster.

This is the same for your spouse. It is not possible to take financial decision without not letting them be aware of it. It is best to create your budgeting plan with each other in order to compare your plans with one another prior to implementing the plans.

It is also necessary to determine the general goal of the money you're saving for. It should be clear in a written explanation of what the objective is and the reason you should begin budgeting in order to meet the desired goal. You and your partner are required to discuss it with each other so that you can be aware of the sacrifices that must be made to achieve the goal.

It could be beneficial to hold weekly family gatherings to provide the opportunity to update all those involved in the process of how you're doing on saving to reach the ultimate goal. If your family has a poor performance on budgeting, you may have a discussion during the meeting about strategies for how your performance can be improved the next time. You can discuss the behavioral modifications that have to be implemented, the adjustments that the family has to implement , as well as other possible solutions for your budgeting concerns.

Chapter 14: The Reasons Why Budgeting is Important?

In everyday life, budgeting method is a method to assist the money get the desired results from every activity. In the event that you've heard it a few times or more, you've heard it a million many times before: BUDGET YOUR FINANCES! Cash counselors and financial specialists have been shouting this mantra from the tops for quite a while.

This is just one of those financial exercises that aren't taught enough. If both your household and you members require security in the financial realm, setting your financial limits is the best option.

Are you still not convinced? Here are six convincing reasons why everyone should set and stick to an expenditure limit.

1. It helps you keep your Focus on the Goal

Spending money helps you to consider your goals over the long term and set out to achieve your goals. If you float around in a haze throughout your life, throwing money at every single object that catches your attention, then by how will you put aside enough cash to buy a car visit Aruba or make an initial installment down on a home?

The pressure of spending forces you to set out your goals put aside the money and monitor your progress and transform your desires into reality. Okay, it's possible to be a bit difficult to realize that the brand new brand new Xbox game or that stunning cashmere sweater you saw in the shop window won't be able to fit in your budget. If you inform yourself that you're saving something to put aside for a different house then it's more straightforward to move and leave the shop without spending a dime.

2. It ensures that you don't spend the money you don't have

Many shoppers spend money they don't have, and we could owe all of it to Mastercards. In fact, the average credit card obligation per household was $2300 in June of 2019, as per an ongoing report by ValuePenguin. Before the advent of plastic, people were able to tell if they were following their means. At the end of the month when they were certain you had the money to pay the bills and stash some reserve funds They were in the right direction. Today, people who abuse and abuse credit cards aren't usually aware of their overspending until they're in the process of suffocating their creditors.

But should you set and stick to a spending plan and stick to it, you won't end up in this precarious situation. You'll be aware of the amount of money you make, the amount you'll be able to through each month, and the sum you're able to save. Of obviously you'll find that making the calculations and keeping track of your financial limitations isn't quite as enjoyable like going on a rash shopping spree. However, look at it this way If your spending-minded friends are scheduled to meet with an obligation advocate at this in the next year then you'll be heading off to enjoy the European trip you've put some aside, or even more importantly, you'll be moving to your new residence.

3. It can lead to a Happi Retirement

Imagine you use your cash in a way that is efficient, then you can reach your financial limit with precision, and do not ever sign a Mastercard obligation. Bravo! However do you not think you've missed something? In addition to being crucial to spend your money smartly now, it's important to save some money to save for the future.

A financial limit will assist you in doing just that. It is essential to include the ventures you make into your financial limits. If you set aside a portion of your income each month to put into the funds in your IRA, 401(k) or other retirement funds In the end, you'll create a comfortable savings. Even though you might have to give up some today, it's justifiable, in spite of all the problems that lie ahead. If you think about it, why not to spend your retirement playing the fairway and making trips to the beach or working as a greeter in the local supermarket to earn some money? Absolutely.

4. It can help you prepare for the possibility of emergencies.

Life is full of abrupt shocks, with some being superior over others. If you are laid off and then get wiped out or damaged, suffer an unplanned separation or an untimely death in your family, it could trigger real financial turmoil. It appears that these problems often occur under the most unfavorable conditions possible when you're broken and cold. This is the reason everyone has a money-saving account for rainy days.

Your budget should contain a hidden stash which is at a of three to a half year's worth of daily expenses. This extra cash will ensure that you do not fall into the depths of obligation following an actual emergency. It will, of course, put aside money to set aside 3 to 5 months per year's worth of daily expenses.

Be careful not to put the bulk of your checks into your reserve account as soon as you can. Include it in your financial limits as well as set realistic goals. begin small. No matter if you set aside the equivalent of $10 to $30 in savings each week, your savings account will grow gradually.

5. It sheds light on bad spending habits

A spending habit can cause you to examine your method to manage your money. You might find yourself using up your cash for things that you don't need to worry about. Are you really paying attention to every single one of those 500 sites in your expensive extended link plan? Do you really require 30 pairs of dark shoes? Planning allows you to review your methods of managing money and shift your focus to goals for your budget.

6. It's better than counting Sheep

The act of following a budget will also help you to get more attentive attention. Have you ever sat about pondering what you would do to handle the bills? People who suffer from restlessness over money issues are allowing their money to manage them. Take back control. When you budget your money wisely, you will never get restless over budgetary concerns once more.

Benefits of budgeting

You have the power to control your money - A financial limit can be a means to ensure you are deliberate in the way you manage and put aside funds. According to some, with the proper planning, you can control your money, not the cash that controls you. Planned spending helps you avoid the stress of abruptly getting used to the absence of resources as you did not initially decide how you would spend the funds. It also lets you decide in the event that you must forgo a short-term expenditures like buying coffee regularly to get some long-term benefit like an excursion on the road or another HDTV.

Focuses your attention on your money goals. You avoid spending excessively on services and items that do not contribute to achieving your financial goals. If you're working with limited resources, planning makes it easier to earn an adequate living. You are aware of what's happening with your money If you have a plan you know how much cash is coming in, the speed at which it is released and where it's going to. Planning helps you not think about the month's close and where your money was. A financial limit allows you to see what you can afford to maximize your purchasing and contribution opportunities and figure out how you can reduce your obligations. It also informs you the things that are important for you, based on the way you divide your resources, how much cash is serving you and how far you're getting to your financial goals.

It helps you organize your investment and spending funds By separating your cash into categories of uses as well as reserve money, budget will help you be aware of which category of use is which part of your money. This makes it easy to alter your spending. The spending limit also serves as a way to gain insight for organizing your receipts, bills, and budget summary. When the majority of your financial exchanges are prepared to answer charge time or loan boss queries, you will save energy and time.

This allows you to decide in advance what your money will do for you.

Allows you to set aside money aside for unexpected and anticipated costs -

Budgeting lets you to plan your budget to save money for emergency expenses.

Allows you to talk with your loved ones regarding cash. If you are sharing your money with family, friends or anyone else an expense limit could be shared about how you spend money as a group. This helps to build a sense of collaboration on monetary basics and helps avoid conflict over how money is spent. The creation of a financial limit couple with your partner in life will avoid conflict and settle the individual differences in how money is spent. Planned spending helps family members share responsibility and accountability.

It gives you a warning of potential problems - If you make your spending plan and have the "major image" take a look, you'll identify potential cash problems prior to the time and can alter your plans prior to the issue arising.

It helps you decide if you're able to fulfill your obligations and what amount - It's not bad in the event that the obligation is vital or you are able to bear the costs. Planned out, you can determine how much of an obligation burden you could effectively handle without being a slave to it or whether the load is justifiable, in spite of all the effort.

It allows you to make extra cash. During planning, you have the possibility to recognize and eliminate unnecessary spending such as penalty charges, late charges, and charges. The seemingly small savings can be found after a while.

Why it is important to budget

Setting up solid budgetary decisions is an essential part of having financial security. One of the options is to plan your expenditure. Planning is a basic and routine tool which can save hundreds, if not many dollars over the long run. You also become more aware of the ways you manage your money and where the money is going.

Reserve funds

You might think that you are constantly all over the world to put aside money this is true. It's not too late to start early. Making sure you have enough cash in the investment accounts is crucial to have a successful financial future. It also allows the user to create a backup plan in the event that you require cash or run out of cash.

Investment funds are always an excellent idea and can help you avoid anxiety and headaches. Furthermore, by taking care of money, you can determine how to stay within your budget and not invest more than you earn.

Backup Plan

The importance of having a "Plan B" is always a good idea. You should never be unreasonably prepared for the life events that are in store and being financially protected is one way to be ready. Major life events could cause the financial burden of getting married or having a child or health-related crisis. When these events occur it is essential to be prepared.

Manage Your Spending

Have you ever been to a shop and you walked in looking for one item, only to walk out three items? Most people have done it, however planning can help limit spending spills. If you are confined to a certain amount of money to spend you'll be able to modify your desires to purchase additional items.

Plan your shopping sprees

If you plan to spend your money isn't a reason to not spend it. A portion of your planning is preparing for huge expenses and extravagant spending is just one of the most frequent ones. Just because you're being savvy on your money does not mean that you should be able to invest all of it.

With planning, you be able an extra cost for certain things you really require without feeling guilty or embarrassed about it. Planning allows you to consider a variety of expensive items every now and then but without impacting your month-to- monthly expenses negatively. You can still spend money and keep track of your bills.

No more late payments

In the event of being late or behind on any payment is not a good indication. If you are late on your installments, it can lead to you being liable and then create more financial problems for you. The planning will prevent you from not paying your installments on time or making late installments on large bills as you already have money set aside for this charge. The spending you make will ensure that every bill is paid on time as it is one of the main requirements of your budget.

Achieving Your Objectives

Setting goals and reaching them is a gratifying process and satisfying. Making a clear and concise budget will allow you to reach your goals reliably and regularly. You'll have the chance to accomplish your goal of putting aside money to purchase a car or going to an extravagant excursion with no hassle since you planned. You will also be able to witness your progress and effort will pay off.

Better Money Habits to Make Money

Change your approach to managing your money can be difficult but planning will help by making small adjustments that can make a difference. As time passes, you will begin to notice shifts in the way you look at your finances your money and the method you use to manage your money. You'll start to realize advantages and will be able to reward yourself for having sound financial habits. In the end, you'll be able to distinguish bad costs from good ones swiftly and be adept at avoiding spending.

When you have to alter your financial habits it is essential to come up with a plan and put it into motion. A plan is useless when you don't implement it into your daily life. Through planning, you'll determine how to settle on smart spending decisions and also save money at the same time.

Chapter 15: Jot Out Your Priorities

On the same worksheet you used to list your objectives (Goal saving Worksheet) It is important to decide and write down the goals that are most important to you.

How do you record your top priorities.

Take note of the lesson you learnt in the article Determine Your Need & What You to that section. Let me demonstrate how to list your top priorities:

Find out the goal that is required to be completed prior to a specific date. If you have to purchase new equipment or complete some improvements in the next 3 months it is best to set it as a top priority. Find out the areas where you can cut to save money now and ensure that you have enough money in three months. Keep in mind that the earlier you begin saving, the more you will save.

Place them in chronological order.Place the most significant goals you would like to achieve first on the list. The first item on the list needs to be accomplished first. You must adhere to your decision today and for the next few months. Be sure that the items listed as foremost, second and third are the most important objectives to your budget. Don't look at your desires on this list particularly if you own something that is indispensable in your daily life.

Set a target date. When will it be required to be completed? Consider taking a step back to look at your present situation. If you can put it off for a while, place the deadline for the project under the longer-term categories. If the projects need to be completed earlier it is best to give them first priority.

Find out how much it costs. Find out the cost for each goal, so you know the amount of amount of money you will need to achieve the objectives. Make sure you have more than you require, in the event that it will cost slightly more than you expected.

Determine how much you will save each month to reach your objective. Based on the money you have you can decide the amount you would like to contribute for each objective. The most important goals should be more funds than the ones with lower priorities.

After you have set your goals The following step involves prioritizing the urgent or important ones. This will help ensure that money will go where our priorities are.

It's all it takes is a just a few minutes of your time and some good self-control. After you have decided on what amount to put aside for each goal and which is most important then you must be your own guide for your future investments and expenses. Your budget won't be able to be successful in the end of the day if you do not follow through.

What is the best time to use it?

The purpose of writing the priorities down is whenever you're tempted to spend money, you're going be hesitant to make a decision because you are aware that it's not in line with your values. That's what you want!

What does this mean for entrepreneurs?

For business owners, this is as crucial as identifying what tasks have to be completed first. In the event that you do not have an action list, I would suggest keeping it updated on a regular basis. Writing your goals for business down with their priority level will help you determine the priorities you should be. When you have several employees, you would like the majority of them to be focused on the things that need to be completed today, and a few of them focusing on what has to be completed later on.

If you're running an enterprise, or are self-employed, that means to complete what is needed to be done now. Do you plan to host an open house one week ahead of the time? Absolutely you aren't. It's the same for your goals. List them out and decide those that are important. So your money will go where it's needed to be.

One of the most effective tips that I can offer is to ensure that you have your check balance in a good state. You shouldn't keep any leftovers! In the event that you have leftovers, place it somewhere else , where an extra bit of food can be helpful. Within your budget it is recommended that you have some money set aside for leisure activities, or else you'll be exhausted.

The earlier you decide what you need to do first, the quicker you will be able to start saving and accumulating the money required to accomplish it happen. I'm unable to determine for you what you should make an investment in but investing will help your business develop. If it does not then it's not an investment.

Be aware of where your money goes , and you'll be able to identify new goals every day.

Here are the advantages of making a list of your priorities

Your money will go wherever you would like it to be. By writing down your top priorities and priorities, you determine the place your money left after you've paid all the bills. Don't waste money on things that don't matter. Your hard-earned cash is used where it's needed! If you're married to a spouse, be sure that she will be delighted that the ideas you've talked about for years are finally taking shape.

You're making progress. You'll no longer be wondering why you've worked for years, but you aren't making progress. In fact, when you establish objectives, when you prioritize them , and then you plans to reach these goals, they're more likely to occur. Each goal you achieve your goals. If these are your personal objectives or business goals to build a great business You are making progress. I am excited just to consider it!

You know the things that matter to you. "I'm aware of what's important to me Jean-Gabriel!" That's true, but how come your money isn't a representation of it? If you can identify them you are giving yourself the opportunity to be able to accept the things you really want. It takes only a few moments, yet the repercussions are enormous. If you do what's necessary, you'll discover new ways of living.

You get more organised. Your goals are similar to those on your list of things to do however, they are more exciting! You organize the things you'd like to achieve whether in your business or life and also when. Planning is the best way to avoid to be a failure. If you come up with a fresh idea or goal you want to achieve then you should immediately note it down and put it as a top priority for the time it has to be accomplished. This changes the way you live your life and, since you are doing more and feel better, you'll are happier. This is always the aim.

Chapter 16: Simple Bargain Shopping Tips Guaranteed to Help You Save Money

Here are a few cheap shopping tips I employ to save money.

Boldness is rewarded

Most of the time, people are often shy. I'm not able to recall how many times I've bought an item at a bargain price at one point but then return to the same shop just a few days later to discover that the item is being sold. If you find something that you like, be sure to inquire whether you can purchase it at the item for a lower price. This is particularly important in the case of clothing stores.

Social-stalk your favorite store

It's not that you become a social on your favorite shop; I'm saying that you follow them on Twitter as well as follow their page on Facebook. Why is this so important when bargain hunts? Since the advent in social media the majority of big retail stores have "gone-social". That means that before they place the discount banners on their glass doors or put an advertisement in the local paper or billboards, they are able to announce the deals to their followers first. By following this method, you can be sure that you're the first you can get there before others rush to grab those bargains that are best value for money products.

Free shipping is the best option for you

One of the biggest drawbacks of shopping online is the shipping costs. In many instances, I've discovered bargains but then went to the checkout only to realize that the shipping costs and the price of purchase is a lot more than I would have paid if purchased the item off the shelves. Although we will explore bargain shopping online in detail I suggest you look for bargains with free shipping, or purchase from stores like Talbots or J crew that offer free shipping on catalogs and online products.

Be aware of the sales tax amount

One method you can take to get around the tax on sales is to purchase from an out-of-state online store and then ship the item. Furthermore, many states provide discounts on sales tax rates on their websites. So, it is recommended to visit the State website to find out what items you are eligible for reduce (sale tax rebate). One good argument and reason is that the majority of States don't tax clothing purchases less than $100. This allows you to take advantage of breaking your big purchase into smaller, below $100 consignments.

Dear Old compare cliche

This topic will pop up frequently in our bargain-hunting lessons. There's no way that to determine how to get the best price without comparing the prices and items in other stores. But, comparing store to store can be stressful, and given that we live in a busy world, you might not have the time for a "store hop" in your search for a bargain; hence searching online is the best alternative. Major retailers across both the U.S as well as the UK have websites. Check out the store's website, and, if you purchase an item, go to the website of its rivals to find out what price they are offering on the identical or similar item. Most of the time you'll find it will reduce your costs. In addition, you can utilize sites like shopstyle.com to find the best prices from stores.

Chapter 17: The Benefits Of Personal Financial Planning

Planning your personal finances may not be necessary for some. Some people do what they want and manage their finances day to day. They don't have a specific and exact plan to keep their financial stability and safety.

There are a myriad of benefits of personal finance planning one can take advantage of. It is all that is required to put these steps in place to achieve the desired results from his financial situation.

Freedom to indulge and indulge

If you are able to make personal financial plan and are capable of sticking to your plan, you are most likely to be able to save funds saved. Security in your finances allows you to indulge in the things you enjoy in your life.

It is not necessary to take money from friends or obtain a loan from a bank to travel, or to purchase the latest device. You are able to indulge in these activities knowing that it won't break the bank.

Be Free of Debt

Certain individuals can be addicted to buying things they love and see but don't need. It can affect your finances particularly if you succumb to the temptation knowing that you will not have the funds to purchase it.

Your finances are also affected when you purchase out of desire knowing that you are saving your money for other things. It is possible to avoid this from happening to you by efficient financial planning for your personal finances.

Planning implies that you have planning to plan for your future. You anticipate things to occur ahead of when they will. This way you take some preventive actions like saving and investing.

If a person puts his cash in a savings account, it earns a little bit of interest each year. This is still a good option than spending all your cash. The best option is to invest.

If you put your money into investing and invest it, you will see a bigger and more satisfying return out of your money. Don't make money for yourself Let your money do the work. This will allow you to remain out of debt and avoid debt.

Be financially secure

The economic landscape is constantly changing in a constant manner. Inflation here and recession everywhere. It is the reason that many people are squeezing every cent they can. They realize that the financial security of their families is at risk.

Every generation is able to reap lower and lower benefits. It will be the time when, as they get older or when they retire, people are still working because they are unable to receive an entire pension. Making a plan for your finances will help you ensure your retirement as well as old age.

Better Results

If you conduct personal financial planning, you'll get more outcomes. It is possible to make your goals happen because you are confident that the goals you set are attainable and achievable.

Set realistic goals you will be able to meet within a specific time. If you are applying for an loan, you will be able to pay it off on time if you have a determine how much you will spend and also save your hard-earned cash.

The importance of planning your finances for personal use is as it ensures that you can make the most of your financial life. You'll be able to make better decisions regarding spending and money. You can purchase things without worrying about whether it will impact your budget and avoid debts you aren't able to pay.

Then, you will be able to determine how you're making use of your cash. Maybe, money makes the world go around. But, with financial planning you are the one to manage your own money, which gives you the power to manage your own world.

Chapter 18: Strategies for Budgeting

If you're a novice to budgeting, the tips in this chapter are sure to aid you. These guidelines will not just aid in aid you in formulating an appropriate budget, but also in adhering to it. I've also provided various budgeting tools that could help you in this.

Tips for budgeting:

One of the main aspect of budgeting to reduce the amount you spend. Most of the time we are prone to overstep our budgets as we spend more than we expected. Therefore, I have provided some suggestions for cutting down on costs in this section.

Develop the ability to adapt

We are certain that we won't be able follow the budget precisely. This is due to the fact that sometimes our expenses could be higher than we anticipated.

Therefore, it is important to keep a flexible mindset when you plan your budget. So, you'll be safe even in the most extreme scenario. If, on the other hand, you are on a budget that is conservative it is easy to get stressed when your expenses go over the budget. Therefore, try to leave some money in an emergency fund for monthly expenses. This money should be used exclusively for emergencies and not for any other purpose. Do not use this amount when you're trying to purchase something that is over and over your monthly requirements and you have already fulfilled your daily luxury requirements. This is for those occasions when you need to purchase something urgent such as a laptop , for instance, because the one you have had for a while was suddenly out of order. Make sure you are prepared for any emergency and be flexible in your budget.

Make room for some fun

The stress of working and having no enjoyment makes every day boring. A budget that doesn't include the costs that you may have to pay to have amusement is boring. If you don't have room for leisure activities within your budget, you'll be disappointed after spending the money to engage in such things. A budget that is conservative isn't going to hinder us from having enjoyment. It is better to plan for these expenses rather than regretting spending. Additionally, if we put the money aside each month to enjoy fun activities and activities, we'll be able to enjoy our time in a controlled manner. In the sample budget that items like "leisure period" as well as "club" funds are included. These are essential for all. There is no reason to cut off socializing because you need to adhere to the budget. You must be entertained for a healthy functioning. Many people do not include these costs in their budgets thinking that they'll adjust. The truth is that nothing will be adjusted unless you are conscious of it.

This is why these expenses are compulsory to be added to your budget each month.

You should not spend more than your income

Don't spend more than you earn. We often borrow money and then spend a few times. The repayment of these debts becomes the next issue. You must bear this in mind when using credit cards to purchase items. Do not exceed your limit or buy more. This can increase the interest rate for the card, as well. Therefore, you should not spend more than and over your earnings. If you are suffering from this kind of issue, you should consider with a partner to stop you from buying unnecessary items. It is important to carry with your budget-friendly plan wherever you go, so that you can know what you will need to spend on something and the places you should be to reduce your spending. If you feel you're nearing the point of overspending, then put your foot down and tell yourself, I'll buy the next month.

The right reasons to borrow

Only borrow if it's intended to fund an investment that is long-term. In this way, the asset can assist you in repaying the debt. For example, if you get a loan for education and you qualify, you'll be able to pay back the loan with the money you earn due to your eligibility. If you decide to purchase a home and you are in a position to pay back the loan using the rental income that you are making. Don't borrow to fund things that won't help you over the course of time. For example, you may borrow money to purchase a vehicle. The value of the vehicle declines over time and an investment will not be profitable if you're doing it by borrowing money. Similar to when you choose to take out a loan to take a luxurious vacation. When you're done with it, you're faced with a huge headache to pay back the loan in time. Don't borrow to pay for something that will not be the price in the long run and you're assured of having a great chance of earning the cash and repaying the loan in full.

Rent

Don't wait until the beginning of each month to pay rent. If you are able to pay cash before the start of the month that follows you can pay your rent before waiting for the beginning of the next. It is advisable to do this in the event that you are worried about paying the rent prior to the beginning of the next month. Failure to pay your rent is something is easy to avoid. If you default, there will be problems of every kind. You'll be living with a bad credit score and may be kicked out. These are not issues you have to worry about, especially if you're just starting your career.

Pay off your mortgage

It's not mandatory to pay only the specified amount toward your mortgage each month. If, in any month you have additional funds you can pay more than is needed for the mortgage. In this way, you'll be able close it earlier and lower the interest portion. Therefore, you should spend at minimum 10 percent more than you normally would each month for your mortgage. You could choose a greater amount in the event that you believe it will make it easier in the end to repay your loan by paying 15% more than you normally contribute toward it. It is essential to create a solid strategy to accomplish this.

Utilities

Make sure you invest in power-saving utilities like fluorescent bulbs. They can reduce your electric bill by a significant amount. Change the temperature of the thermostat to decrease heating and cooling expenses. The use of ceiling fans will assist in reducing your electric bill. These are a one-time purchase that will save you several dollars in the near future.

Therefore, allocate a portion from your savings budget in order to pay for of these costs.

Transportation expenses

It is best to complete multiple tasks in one journey. In this way, you will cut down on fuel usage and thus reduce the amount that you spend on gas. It is also a great method to control your time.

Utility budgeting:

Make use of one of the following strategies to keep an eye on your spending and to follow your budget:

Pen and notebook

While it's not as easy as it appear, in reality all you require is a notebook, and a pen to record every expense and income. It is also possible to keep an additional column to record savings you earn. Although these are the least costly ways to keep your financial records but the possibility of losing it is present. If you are planning to make time to plan your budget, ensure that you've got these in your bag and that you aren't waiting around unprepared to go about it or scramble in the last minute to discover them.

Spreadsheet

A simple Excel spreadsheet will do in a way that is amazing. It also assists in avoiding mistakes that are made manually and you'll be able perform complicated calculations in a matter of seconds , and receive the most accurate figures. The benefit of using a spreadsheet is that once you have create the formulas for certain fields, you do not have to revise the entire process regardless of changes to the formula. Therefore, you should begin by creating an excel spreadsheet with a finalized formula to track your budget. You can then utilize it every month to change the numbers within it. It is possible to save it across all your devices, and then forward your copy to yourself. The goal is to keep it available each month to complete the information and create the budget easily.

Financial Software

There are many financial softwares on the market including Microsoft money as well as Quicken. These are the most advanced versions of your spreadsheet, and are capable of keeping track of your income and expenditures in a more efficient method. It helps you keep track of your bank and investment accounts too. You'll be able to examine at all your accounts, and you will know the amount of money you have and where it is. But, it could be very risky in the event that someone else gets an access point to the computer. They could get your financial details in a flash.

Online Software

Nowadays, there are several versions of online programs to help you track your finances and keep track of your budget. A majority of these are free , and the other are available at a low cost. Because they're online and accessible from any device, you'll be able to access your figures from any location. You can make changes to your expenses instantly without delay. It is possible to directly connect all of your bank accounts and make them one. You'll have a better chance at keeping track of your expenses and don't have to fumble through the streets with a pen and paper. You'll have everything in your reach and be able to quickly make changes to any and all items connected to your budget and financials. However, not all people would feel comfortable making changes to their financial records on the internet. There is the risk of fraud, as well as identity theft. Be wary of sites that are not trustworthy and select one that is dependable and is reputable to ensure that your funds as well as your identity is protected. It is possible to ask your friends for suggestions to ensure you are secure.

Chapter 19: Saving Money

The next step to manage your budget is to conserve money.When you implement the techniques discussed in the previous chapter, you'll notice an improvement in the amount you pay for the items that you typically buy each month.

As you become inventive in the ways you can purchase the things that you require and want at a lower cost You will need to deposit the money you've saved in your savings account at the bank.

For instance, if you usually spend an amount of $500 for groceries every month , but you begin employing strategies to cut costs , and then you discover that you can now purchase the same items you normally purchase for $480, you'll deposit the savings of $20 each month to your savings account.Now the amount may seem like much , but you'll be looking to feel satisfaction that you've been able to save money in any amount even when you are in the burden of debt.

Other methods you can employ to save money, or to spend, is to sell items from your home that you no longer require or have grown out of.You can offer these items through a yard sale or even sell them online.The thing is that you'll need to sell items that you are sure you never will ever use or objects you grew out of.

You may also use any gift cards given to you, specifically things that you can use to purchase items for your household , and then purchase with card instead of cash.The money you save can be transferred into the savings accounts in your account.

If you're also noticing that you dine at restaurants every day for lunch during work, you can bring lunch to work and conserve the money you spend eating out or buying a cup of coffee less each day.

Other strategies you can employ to save money are:

Sell or auction off items you no longer require or do not want on the internet.

Carpooling to work

Make use of gift cards that you've been gifted to purchase household goods instead

Make use of Coupons and promo codes to reduce costs

Eat out less

Find a side-job on weekends

Make sure you are following the right driving habits to obtain lower insurance rates or the chance to receive a rebate check

If you own a credit card with rewards you can use the card to purchase household goods and pay them off in a hurry. charge

Make use of rebate saving apps to exchange points into gift cards

Contribute to the company's retirement plan to earn money and not be assessed tax (keep in mind that your post tax earnings may be lower).

Make sure you have pocket change to take pennies or change people to are lying on the floor

Take home household items, particularly if they are on the clearance shelves at your preferred shops

Purchase generic brands of your favourite items I guarantee you that they're exactly the same as famous brands.

Purchase in Bulk You must determine this prior to purchasing, but buying in bulk could result in cost savings.

Purchase gasoline at stations that are associated with grocery stores.Usually grocery stores provide you with gas discounts.Sometimes the discounts could be as much as 50 cents off per gallon, which can accumulate over the course of.

As you begin to cut costs, you'll see how much money save will accumulate over time.In the time, you will be able to reduce the amount you've saved and put the funds to pay off your debts.

Chapter 20: Effective Debt Management

The debt is among the most significant clogs on the investment process and saving.

Many people want to begin saving money and investing, but are entangled in too much debt that it becomes nearly impossible to put aside any funds at the time of the end of the month.

The answer is to create an appropriate budget and repayment plan that will handle your daily savings and monthly installments.

Here are some steps you need to take to efficiently manage and pay off your debts and still commit to your savings and investing plan.

Be aware of the amount you have to pay: First create the list of all your creditors. Then, you can take a complete picture of who you owe and how much you have to pay.

Stop Getting More Debts at this point it is time to stop accumulating debt. Be aware of what you earn and allow it to be enough to meet your needs. Beware of things you can't afford, unless obviously it's a matter of life or death. It is important to only take out loans or make loans in the event of a medical emergency. Other things can be left to.

Tip: You can limit the amount you're exposed to risk arising from health problems by purchasing the health insurance coverage or putting aside a fund for emergencies to cushion you in the event that you're facing financial difficulties.

Make a bill payment calendar Paying late charges can attract interest that can eventually add to your debts. Therefore, you should create bill payment calendars which allows you to keep track of the date when bills are due, to be paid them off early.

Choose which debts to pay off first Start by paying off the credit card debts due these high-interest rates. Take care to pay off debts with high interest first before proceeding to pay other bills with low interest.

Make a commitment of 20% of your income to bill repayment You should begin with 20 percent of your income each month to pay off all obligations until you've wiped the debt completely.

Chapter 21: Staying out Of Debt

One of the most effective methods to control the burden of debt is to keep it out of it. But, sometimes, debt are not a possibility to avoid and, in the event that you are in debt this can have an impact on your finances.

If you already have a mortgage on your home or car, as well as certain bank loans, you should include them as part of your financial plan. Numerous banks and large corporations who offer car and home loans are able to receive payments through bank-to-bank transfer. For example with your permission the accounting department at your business can have loans automatically deducted each month from your paycheck and sent to the company in question. This way it is not necessary to fret about allocating funds for every type of loan, and you don't need to manually submit your payment. When you get your paycheck your monthly loan payments are already deducted, and the remaining amount is what you will need to plan for the household budget. It is also important to keep your track of every payment that you're paying to be aware of the amount of balance you have and the amount of additional installments you'll have to make.

A lot of people also end up in the debt trap due to credit card. The plastic money is quite tempting to spend. By simply swiping, you can purchase anything that catches your attention. There's a credit limit for each card, but it's not a great help to those trying to stick to a budget. The credit card industry is known for their high interest rates which means that even a few accidental purchases can put you with a debt that lasts for years. Numerous credit card owners receive monthly interest for their purchases but not the actual amount of debt. In the meantime, the total credit balance grows until the person who owns the card is having problems in clearing the debt. If you consider the possibility that people who use plastic money have the option of having several credit card accounts that can be used at once this can be an ideal way to get yourself in an abyss and end up by debt. If you think you're in danger of engaging in this kind of behavior in your spending If you want to stay clear of this, stay away on credit cards. If you have to own one, keep it in the house and use it only for emergencies. Contrary to utility bills that are fixed in amount, credit cards can increase in time. The more you are spending on clearing your debts more, the larger it grow. This can seriously mess up even the most efficient financial plans.

It is also not uncommon to borrow money from their friends and relatives particularly when times are difficult. However, this is the purpose of having the ability to budget. By having a budget, you can prevent you from going into debt and having to borrow. With a solid budget that you have in place, you'll always have enough cash to cover your needsand other expenses too. In reality, if you've borrowed money from relatives or friends this is the right time to set aside money to repay them. As you did when you set up an account line item in your budget for "groceries" as well as "utilities" then you need to make a line item for "paying the Uncle Mickey," and put the money in that account each month.

If you establish your own budget and stick to it, you will stay out of debt. Regain the control over your finances and live a more balanced life. Set a goal for yourself to be debt free and then stay clear from it afterward!

Chapter 22: Setting Financial Goals

In the first and second chapters of this guide were drawn up with two reasons to educate you of what you require in order to manage your finances and to allow you to gain a clear picture of your financial situation. Once you've gotten a sense of how much you can apply to your loans without having to compromise your lifestyle or create a new loan account, it's time to establish your plan with objectives. This chapter will show you how to achieve this.

In the case of goal-setting You can't get around this acronym SMARTER. This acronym describes the ideal goals to be that is specific, quantifiable, feasible, realistic, assess and revise. These two elements are vital because , as you advance in life, it is inevitable to be faced with choices that impact your objectives. This is why you should be able to adapt to changes.

Set goals that are specific

To create a specific goal you can break it down into three broad categories: medium-term, short-term and long-term. Both the short-term and medium-term objectives are goals in and of themselves, but they serve a purpose. That means they're steps towards the achievement of your long-term objective. This is an illustration of a goal statement:

Goal for the short-term: to reduce your monthly expenses

Long-term goal: To reduce costs in one year

Long-term goal is to get my vehicle loan paid off.

The goal setting process should be measurable.

To be able to measure your goals it is necessary to establish an established baseline. This will tell you the degree to which you've been succeeding in achieving your target within the timeframe provided. In order to make these three objectives above quantifiable, you could modify them as follows:

Goal for the short-term: To save $400 every month.

Long-term goal: To reduce the cost by $4800 by the end of the year.

Long-term goal is to pay my auto loan balance within 3 years.

Setting goals that are achievable

They are only possible when you have a clear plan of action to reach the goals. If we consider the three goals mentioned in the previous paragraph as an example, the short-term and medium-term goals are the action plans which make the long-term goal feasible. So, you may alter the goals in the following manner:

Goal: Short-term goal: save $400 every month by setting up an automatic transfer of funds from my pay account to my savings account.

Long-term goal: To save $4800 in this year by not taking withdrawals from my savings account.

Long-term goal: repay my auto loan account in three years by putting funds into my savings account.

Making goals realistic

The element of realistic in financial goals is the practicality. This aspect is contingent on the possibility of achieving the objective. It is said that when a goal isn't achievable, it's not feasible enough. What can we do to ensure that our goals are realistic? This is by taking into consideration the length of time as well as other variables that could impact our commitment. If, for instance, we are considering changing jobs, we may not save money for a long time until we are employed. So, if we don't expect any difficulties in the attaining our goals The goal statements remain the same:

Short-term goal: save $400 a month by making an automatic transfer from my account for payroll to my savings account.

Goal for the medium term: to save $4800 in this year by not taking withdrawals from my savings account.

Long-term goal is to complete the repayment of my auto loan account in three years by putting funds into my savings account.

Making goals time-bound

Since we already include an element of time in our goals ($400 every month, $4800 over 12 months and loan repayment over three years) We can now set our goals as time-bound by identifying that we'd like to begin working. The goals then will be:

Goal for the short term: To save $400 a month by making an automatic transfer from my pay account to my savings account beginning the next month.

Goal for the medium term: to save $4800 over this year by staying away from withdrawing funds from my savings account beginning the month following.

Long-term goal: repay my auto loan account in three years, by putting funds in my account for savings from the month following.

Re-evaluating and assessing your financial goals

We've now created three goals statements based on the SMART framework, it's time to think about the challenges we might face on the way and how we could make use of these challenges to assess the value for our objectives. In this respect it is essential to have a lot of flexibility is necessary not just for our goals but also for us.

For instance, in the light of the goal statements we're making, what would we do in the event that we experience an emergency and need to take an emergency withdrawal out of the savings accounts? If the interest rate for the auto loan is changed how many changes are we able to make to our savings amount? save? What happens if we get cuts in pay? How will we affect our goal savings every month?

There are numerous possibilities that could happen within the span of three years. Therefore how can we handle such modifications and alter our plan even if that means changing the three-year plan into the four-year plan? What happens if we eventually pay off all our obligations?

Chapter 23: Resetting Your Eyes on your future wealth

It might not be obvious that the actions you're taking to save money and create wealth and prosperity is benefiting immediately away.Gaining riches and security isn't easy things to attain in the short term or right away.However when you look at the larger view, it may inspire you to keep going on your path you've taken to change your habits.In this section I'll offer some ideas about how to consider your future instead of focusing on your the present circumstances.

Set a goal for the future.

If you don't have a plan that you can see, then your efforts will likely fail.So prior to going to the hassle of trying to alter how you manage your money, consider what the final outcome will be for you.What do you wish to achieve from your wealth? When you have an answer that you can trust, concentrate on it when you are implementing strategies to increase your wealth!

Imagine where you'd like to be five years from now.

Make a plan for what you want your life to be in the coming five years.It could not go this way however, if you have objectives and goals to build financial success, focusing in the coming five years can provide the motivation you'll need to continue exploring different strategies to make money.

Find ways to keep yourself motivated throughout the course of your journey

Every time we attempt something, it can fail.Don't let this hinder your ultimate goal.Find strategies to maintain moving when you feel as if you're doing things wrong.You may have to keep reiterating your goals a few occasions to succeed.Have something to encourage you to keep going even when things aren't going as well as they should.

Continue to look for ways to save money.

I'm just scratching the topic with this book.There are many ways you can be taught to save money and build wealth.Continue to seek out these methods and incorporate these into your routine.You may find something that isn't discussed here that is the most important factor to success.

Concentrate on the final outcome instead of the present circumstances

It can be difficult to begin and stay moving when you feel as if there's no way to achieve money in your life.Don't dwell on the negatives in this moment.Focus only on your positive final result and let it help you through difficult times.

Take a look at the successful and determine what is working for them.

Try using wealthy and successful individuals as models for your role models.It's been observed that a lot of the most wealthy people are among the top penny-pinchers out there.Try finding out what contributed to their success and wealth.The"rags to riches" philosophy is a reality throughout the lives of many people because of the way they dealt with their money, even though they had only a small amount.

The idea of knowing what your final objective is to continue working, even if you think that nothing is happening from it.Keep your sights towards the end of the road and overcome the hurdles when they arise.

Chapter 24: Possibilities Of Passive Income

The term "passive income" refers to income is earned when you are not directly or in any way involved. One example source of earnings is the rental home, where you earn a particular amount of money each monthly from your property but you are not working on the property day-to-day. This type of income can be tax deductible as is passive income. Dividends and interest earned from certain types of investment are also considered to be passive income.

A passive income can be extremely beneficial in numerous ways. If you lose money from a passive venture, such as this, only the amount of money you make are lost, not the revenue or the your initial investment in general. It is possible to earn income from a vacant rental property, however the property will be exactly the same.

These are some income passive options you can think of in order to earn an income for oneself to improve personal financial stability:

Investing in eBooks

The process of creating an eBook may appear to be a lot of work and effort at first, however after the hard part is accomplished, you'll be able make a little income through it for a long period of time. eBooks can be offered via your website, or in partnership with other websites selling similar content to that you offer on your eBook. Be sure to create an excellent eBook, and then market it properly and then see the amount of revenue it could make you over the several years.

The idea of establishing a lending club

People are always searching for a loan provider, particularly for short-term loans. You could be the lender that they call upon whenever they need financial protection, and you can earn some money from the interest that you will be charging for loans you offer.

Real estate investment

A new and improved real property you can always lease or rent out is an excellent method to earn steady income for a long time. You must ensure that it is well-managed and maintained and it should last for a long period of time.

Marketing through affiliates

It is a great method to earn money passively for a period of time. The trick is to set up a website which you promote the products of certain companies. They are willing to pay you specific amount of money or commission once sales have been completed. Businesses are always seeking opportunities to market their goods so you'll never be in the absence of customers.

Chapter 25: How To Create A Budget to Achieve Your Aims?

If you're struggling in the area of debt, creating your own budget could prove to be very helpful. It is important to ensure to make an appropriate budget. Many people commit the mistake of sitting down, taking a look at all their expenses , and then trying to cut them down by a percentage that isn't important like 10 percent or 20%.

Where should you begin?

The best place to begin when creating the budget is to establish your long and short-term goals. Your short-term goals should be those you're likely to achieve within a year or less. If, for instance, you're dealing with debt, the best goal is to eliminate it. The key is to select the goal that you're likely to meet and are able to track on a regular basis.

Next, define your long-term goal or goals. It could be to purchase an apartment or send your children to college , or to save for retirement.

Now that you've got that information, you can

If you've determined what your objectives are and what you want to achieve, you'll know the amount you'll have to save every month , and you'll be able to begin formulating a budget plan to take you to that goal. As an instance, a short-term objective could be to save $200 every month to pay off debt and another $100 towards an investment goal for the future, such as to save for retirement.

Keep track of all your expenses

The next step is to record all of your expenses for at minimum 30 days. It is possible to do this the old-fashioned way by using notespads and pencils or, if you own smartphones there are numerous budgeting and expense tracking applications that are available. The two most well-known apps are Mint (mint.com) as well as you Need A Budget. I would recommend using one of these budgeting apps since it will remove a large portion of the task of preparing and adhering the budget your shoulders. For instance the majority of them automatically break your spending down into appropriate categories such as transportation, entertainment, food and medical costs, insurance and so on.

You can clearly determine the where your money is going, you can see where it's going.

If you are able to see the direction your money is taking and where it is going, then comes the most important aspect. You must figure out the best places to cut the expenses needed to reduce your expenses enough to be below your income level so to allow you to save up for your goals.

Going back to our previous example, if your objectives are to save $300 per month, you'll need to reduce your expenses at least to $300 less than your income.

Conclusion

I hope that this book was helpful in getting you started using a budgeting method.

The next thing to do is follow the strategies laid out in the book. Keep track of your performance and find areas to make improvements. Budgeting is only able to make an impact on your daily life if you do it consistently over an extended period of time.

If you are patient enough you'll be able to meet your financial goals, one at one time. When you've reached all of your short-term goals, then you are able to begin accumulating funds for an early retirement as well as other long-term financial goals.